everyday Comprehension
Intervention Activities

Table of Contents

Using Everyday Comprehension Intervention Activities

Reading with full text comprehension is the ultimate goal of all reading instruction. Students who read the words but don't comprehend them aren't really reading at all. Research has shown that explicit comprehension strategy instruction helps students understand and remember what they read, which allows them to communicate what they've learned with others and perform better in testing situations.

Although some students master comprehension strategies easily during regular classroom instruction, many others need additional re-teaching opportunities to master these essential strategies. The Everyday Intervention Activities series provides easy-to-use, five-day intervention units for Grades K–5. These units are structured around a research-based Model-Guide-Practice-Apply approach. You can use these activities in a variety of intervention models, including Response to Intervention (RTI).

Getting Started

In just five simple steps, Everyday Comprehension Intervention Activities provides everything you need to identify students' comprehension needs and to provide targeted, research-based intervention.

1. PRE-ASSESS to identify students' comprehension needs.

Use the pre-assessment on the CD-ROM to identify the strategies your students need to master.

2. MODEL the strategy.

Every five-day unit targets a specific strategy. On Day 1, use the teacher prompts and reproducible activity to introduce and model the strategy.

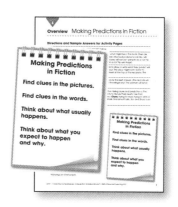

Day 1

3. GUIDE PRACTICE and APPLY.

Use the reproducible practice activities for Days 2, 3, and 4 to build students' understanding of, and proficiency with, the strategy.

Day 2

Day 3

Day 4

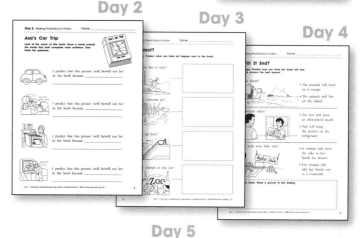

Day 5

4. MONITOR progress.

Administer the Day 5 reproducible assessment to monitor each student's progress and to make instructional decisions.

5. POST-ASSESS to document student progress.

Use the post-assessment on the CD-ROM to measure students' progress as a result of your interventions.

Standards-Based Comprehension Strategies in Everyday Intervention Activities

The comprehension strategies found in the Everyday Intervention Activities series are introduced developmentally and spiral from one grade to the next based on curriculum standards across a variety of states. The chart below shows the comprehension strategies addressed at each grade level in this series.

Comprehension Strategy	Strategy Definition	K	1	2	3	4	5
Make Predictions	Determine what might happen next in a story or nonfiction piece. Predictions are based on information presented in the text.	✔	✔	✔	✔	✔	✔
Identify Sequence of Events	Determine the order of events for topics such as history, science, or biography. Determine the steps to make or do something.	✔	✔	✔	✔	✔	✔
Analyze Story Elements	Analyze the setting and plot (problem/solution) in a fiction text.	✔	✔	✔	✔	✔	✔
Analyze Character	Analyze story characters based on information and on clues and evidence in the text, including description, actions, dialogue, feelings, and traits.	✔	✔	✔	✔	✔	✔
Identify Main Idea and Supporting Details	Determine what the paragraph, page, or chapter is mostly about. Sometimes the main idea is stated and sometimes it is implied. Students must choose details that support the main idea, not "just any detail."	✔	✔	✔	✔	✔	✔
Summarize	Take key ideas from the text and put them together to create a shorter version of the original text. Summaries should have few, if any, details.	✔	✔	✔	✔	✔	✔
Compare and Contrast	Find ways that two things are alike and different.	✔	✔	✔	✔	✔	✔
Identify Cause and Effect	Find things that happened (effect) and why they happened (cause). Text may contain multiple causes and effects.	✔	✔	✔	✔	✔	✔
Make Inferences	Determine what the author is suggesting without directly stating it. Inferences are usually made during reading and are made from one or two pieces of information from the text. Students' inferences will vary but must be made from the evidence in the text and background knowledge.	✔	✔	✔	✔	✔	✔
Draw Conclusions	Determine what the author is suggesting without directly stating it. Conclusions are made during and after reading, and are made from multiple (3+) pieces of information from the text. Students' conclusions will vary but must be drawn from the evidence in the text and background knowledge.		✔	✔	✔	✔	✔
Evaluate Author's Purpose	Determine why the author wrote the passage or used certain information. A book can have more than one purpose. Purposes include to entertain, to inform, and to persuade.			✔	✔	✔	✔
Analyze Text Structure and Organization	Determine the text structure to better understand what the author is saying and to use as research when text must be analyzed.			✔	✔	✔	✔
Use Text Features to Locate Information	Use text features (bullets, captions, glossary, index, sidebars) to enhance meaning.			✔	✔	✔	✔
Use Graphic Features to Interpret Information	Use clues from graphic features (charts, maps, graphs) to determine what is not stated in the text or to enhance meaning.			✔	✔	✔	✔
Distinguish and Evaluate Facts and Opinions	Recognize objective statements of fact and subjective opinions within a nonfiction text.					✔	✔
Make Judgments	Use facts from the text and prior knowledge and beliefs to make and confirm opinions about the characters or situations.					✔	✔

Everyday Comprehension Intervention Activities Grade 3 • ©2010 Newmark Learning, LLC

Using Everyday Intervention for RTI

According to the National Center on Response to Intervention, RTI "integrates assessment and intervention within a multi-level prevention system to maximize student achievement and to reduce behavior problems." This model of instruction and assessment allows schools to identify at-risk students, monitor their progress, provide research-proven interventions, and "adjust the intensity and nature of those interventions depending on a student's responsiveness."

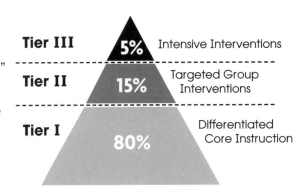

RTI models vary from district to district, but the most prevalent model is a three-tiered approach to instruction and assessment.

The Three Tiers of RTI	Using Everyday Intervention Activities
Tier I: Differentiated Core Instruction • Designed for all students • Preventive, proactive, standards-aligned instruction • Whole- and small-group differentiated instruction • Ninety-minute, daily core reading instruction in the five essential skill areas: phonics, phonemic awareness, comprehension, vocabulary, fluency	• Use whole-group comprehension mini-lessons to introduce and guide practice with comprehension strategies that all students need to learn. • Use any or all of the units in the order that supports your core instructional program.
Tier II: Targeted Group Interventions • For at-risk students • Provide thirty minutes of daily instruction beyond the ninety-minute Tier I core reading instruction • Instruction is conducted in small groups of three to five students with similar needs	• Select units based on your students' areas of need (the pre-assessment can help you identify these). • Use the units as week-long, small-group mini-lessons.
Tier III: Intensive Interventions • For high-risk students experiencing considerable difficulty in reading • Provide up to sixty minutes of additional intensive intervention each day in addition to the ninety-minute Tier I core reading instruction • More intense and explicit instruction • Instruction conducted individually or with smaller groups of one to three students with similar needs	• Select units based on your students' areas of need. • Use the units as one component of an intensive comprehension intervention program.

Overview   Making Predictions in Fiction

Directions and Sample Answers for Activity Pages

Day 1	See "Provide a Real-World Example" below.
Day 2	Discuss the book cover. Ask students to predict what might be in the book. Then ask them to complete the correct sentences. (will be—the book is about a car trip; will be—people on a car trip often stop to take pictures; will not be—people on a car trip do not usually go to a library; will be—people on a car trip use maps)
Day 3	Read and discuss each page. Then ask students to draw or write what they predict will happen next. (The boy might run to catch the bus. The duck might swim faster to catch up with the other ducks. The girls might meet at the top of the escalator. The kids might visit the chimps first.)
Day 4	Read and discuss each page. Ask students to circle the best answer. (The animals will live on the island. Dad will hang the picture on the refrigerator. The woman will serve the cake to her family for dessert.)
Day 5	Read the story together. Ask students to fill in the missing clues and prediction in the chart. Afterward, meet individually with students to discuss their results. Use their responses to plan further instruction and review. (**Clues:** trying to read, trying to drink a cup of tea, trying to rest. **Prediction:** Mom will ask Grandma if Sally, Sol, and Snout can come over for a while so she can relax.)

Provide a Real-World Example

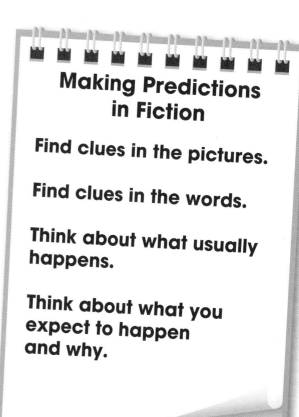

Making Predictions in Fiction

Find clues in the pictures.

Find clues in the words.

Think about what usually happens.

Think about what you expect to happen and why.

◆ Hand out the Day 1 activity page.

◆ **Say:** *My neighbors love biking. The whole family goes on biking trips whenever they can. I can usually predict—or make a good guess about—what they will do on the weekends. What do you predict my neighbors will do this weekend?*

◆ Allow time for students to respond. Then ask them to look at the pictures and color the picture that matches their prediction.

◆ **Say:** *I have another neighbor. He has many antiques in his house. He collects the antiques from yard sales, flea markets, and auctions. What do you predict he will do this weekend? Color the picture that matches your prediction. Then draw a picture. Show what you predict you might do this weekend.*

◆ Explain that students can also predict, or make a good guess, when they read stories. Write the following on chart paper:

This Weekend

Listen. Then color the picture in each row that shows your prediction.

What will you do this weekend? Draw your prediction below.

Asa's Car Trip

Look at the cover of this book. Draw a circle around
the words that best complete each sentence. Then
finish the sentence.

I predict that this picture (will be/will not be)
in the book because _____

_____ .

I predict that this picture (will be/will not be)
in the book because _____

_____ .

I predict that this picture (will be/will not be)
in the book because _____

_____ .

I predict that this picture (will be/will not be)
in the book because _____

_____ .

What's Next?

Read the page. Predict what you think will happen next in the book.

Oh no! The bus is here!

Where did everyone go?

I found it up here!

They have chimps at this zoo!

How Will It End?

**Read the page. Predict how you think the book will end.
Draw a circle around the best answer.**

Look! Land ahead!

- The animals will leave on a voyage.

- The animals will live on the island.

How was school today?

- The boy will have an after-school snack.

- Dad will hang the picture on the refrigerator.

Good luck with your bake sale!

- A woman will serve the cake to her family for dessert.

- The woman will take her family out to a restaurant.

Choose one book. Draw a picture of the ending.

Assessment

Read the passage. Write the clues. Then write what you predict Mom will do.

Mom was trying to read.

"I can't find my favorite red shirt," called Sally.

Mom put her book aside. "I'll help you find it," she said.

Mom was trying to drink a cup of tea.

"I need a snack," called Sol. "What can I have?"

Mom put her tea aside. "I'll help you look for something," she said.

Mom was trying to rest in the shade.

"Woof! Woof!" barked Snout, putting his paws on the hammock.

"So much for resting!" said Mom.

Mom called Grandma. "Are you busy this afternoon?" she asked.

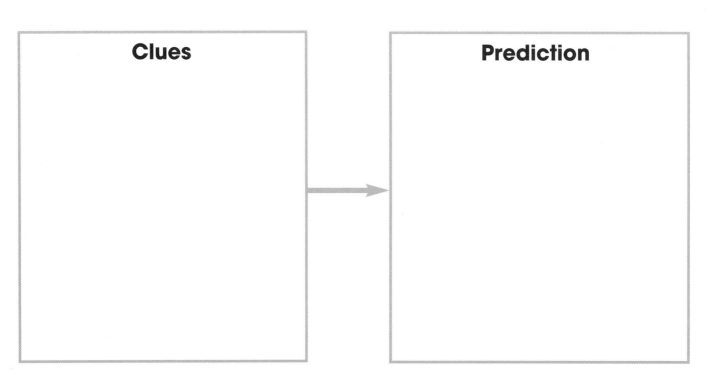

Clues	**Prediction**

Overview Making Predictions in Nonfiction

Directions and Sample Answers for Activity Pages

Day 1	See "Provide a Real-World Example" below.
Day 2	Discuss the book cover. Ask students to predict what might be in the book. Then ask them to complete the correct sentences. (will be—the children are from pioneer days; will not be—there were no computers in pioneer days; will be—people in covered wagons saw many buffalo; will not be—people did not build highways until they started driving cars)
Day 3	Read and discuss each page. Then ask students to draw or write what they predict will happen next. (Baby birds might begin to hatch. A gardener might water the plants. The girl might load groceries into the bike basket. The tree's branches might be empty.)
Day 4	Read and discuss each page. Then ask students to circle the best answers. (ask readers to remember all the ways to stay safe in water; show a picture made entirely of different types of triangles; show a chart summarizing what readers have learned about the eight planets; show what a car of the future might look like)
Day 5	Read the poster together. Ask students to predict what will happen when people read the poster. Afterward, meet individually with students to discuss their results. Use their responses to plan further instruction and review. (**Evidence:** only $1, special shampoo, treats, dog will look great. **Prediction:** Many people will bring their dogs to the dog wash.)

Provide a Real-World Example

◆ Hand out the Day 1 activity page.

◆ **Ask:** *Let's think about school. We usually do certain things on certain days of the week. What do we usually do on Mondays? What do you predict we will do next Monday? Use what you know to predict—or make a good guess about—what we will do.*

◆ Allow time for students to draw or write their predictions.

◆ Repeat the process with the other days of the week.

◆ Invite students to share their predictions with a partner. Then explain that they can also make predictions when they read. Write the following on chart paper:

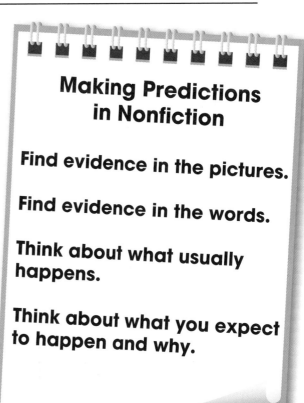

Making Predictions in Nonfiction

Find evidence in the pictures.

Find evidence in the words.

Think about what usually happens.

Think about what you expect to happen and why.

Next Week

Draw or write your prediction for each day.

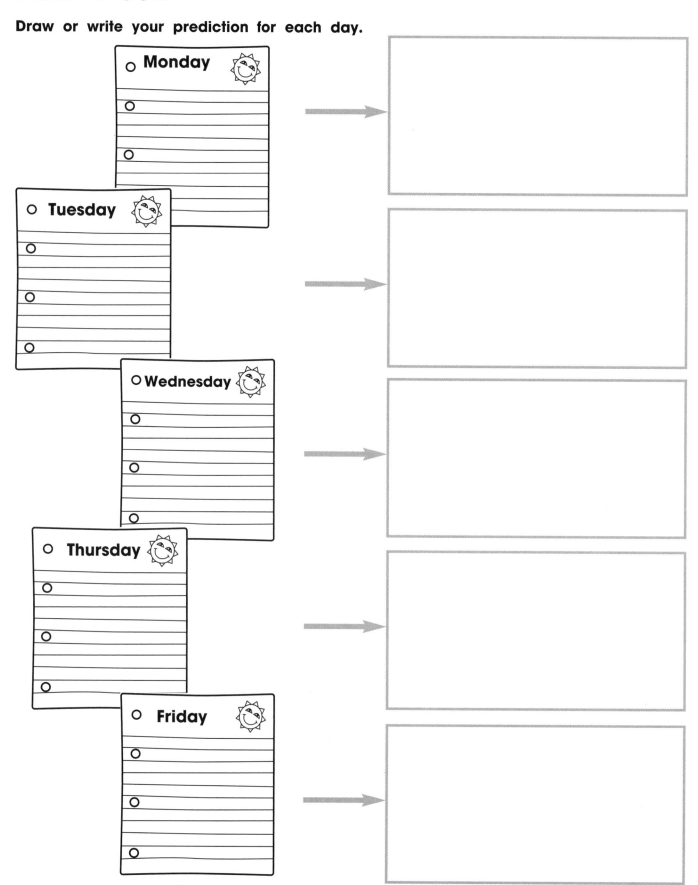

Wagon Train West

Look at the cover of this book. Draw a circle around the words that best complete each sentence. Then finish the sentence.

I predict that this picture (will be/will not be) in the book because _____

_____.

I predict that this picture (will be/will not be) in the book because _____

_____.

I predict that this picture (will be/will not be) in the book because _____

_____.

I predict that this picture (will be/will not be) in the book because _____

_____.

Now What?

Read the page. Predict what you think will happen next in the book.

Mother birds stay with their eggs.

Gardeners must do many things to care for their vegetable plants.

Many people ride their bikes to the store to help the environment.

In autumn, leaves turn different colors and fall from the trees.

The End

Read the page. Predict how you think the book will end. Draw a circle around the best answer.

Never dive into shallow water. Always check the depth first.

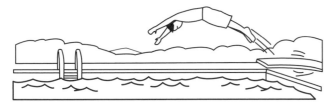

The author will . . .

- ask readers to remember all the ways to stay safe in water

- explain why swimming is the best sport

All triangles have three sides and three angles. The sides and angles can be different sizes.

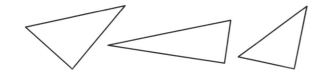

The author will . . .

- teach readers how to draw a circle

- show a picture made entirely of different types of triangles

---

Our solar system has eight planets. The planets travel around the sun.

The author will . . .

- show a chart summarizing what readers have learned about the eight planets

- ask readers if they would like to visit the moon someday

Have you ever seen a car like this? The first cars didn't look much like the cars of today!

The author will . . .

- explain how cars work

- show what a car of the future might look like

Assessment

Read the poster. Write the evidence. Then predict what you think will happen.

Wagging Tail Dog Wash

Only $1 per dog

Special scented shampoo

Treats for good dogs

Your dog will look GREAT!

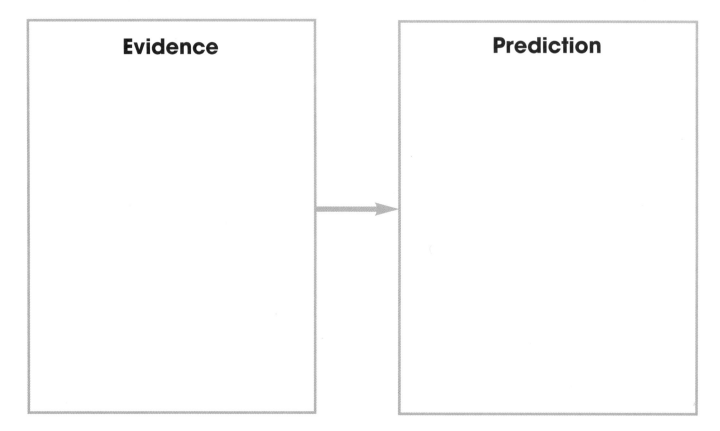

Evidence

Prediction

Overview Identifying Sequence of Events in Fiction

Directions and Sample Answers for Activity Pages

Day 1	See "Provide a Real-World Example" below.
Day 2	Discuss the pictures. Then ask students to cut out the pictures, put them in the correct order, and glue them onto another sheet of paper. (girl jumping rope by herself, another girl joins her, two more girls join them, all four play together)
Day 3	Read and discuss the story. Then help students draw lines to show the correct order. (floats, marching band, flag team, clowns, Gramma)
Day 4	Read and discuss the story. Then ask students to number the pictures in the correct order. (3, 4, 2, 5, 1)
Day 5	Read the story together. Ask students to fill in the graphic organizer. Afterward, meet individually with students to discuss their results. Use their responses to plan further instruction and review. (clean room, wash dishes, rake grass, make lunch, dust and vacuum, play games)

Provide a Real-World Example

◆ Hand out the Day 1 activity page.

◆ **Say:** *One day I ran some errands after school. First, I stopped at the library to return some books. Next, I went to the bank. Then, I bought groceries. Finally, I bought a plant at the greenhouse. I did all these things in a certain order, or sequence. First I did one thing, then another, and another, and another.*

◆ Ask students to look at the pictures and write the number 1 to show what you did first. Repeat with the other three events. Then invite them to share other things people do in a certain order.

◆ Explain that students can also find a sequence of events when they read stories. Write the following on chart paper:

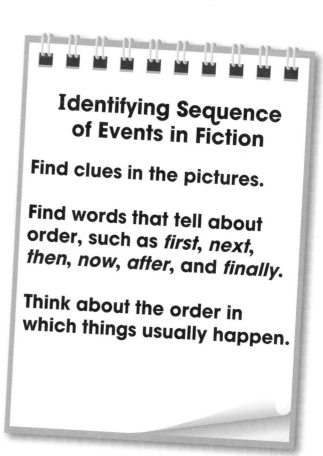

Identifying Sequence of Events in Fiction

Find clues in the pictures.

Find words that tell about order, such as *first, next, then, now, after,* and *finally.*

Think about the order in which things usually happen.

After School

Listen. Then number each picture in the correct order.

Jump Rope

Look at the pictures. What story can they tell?

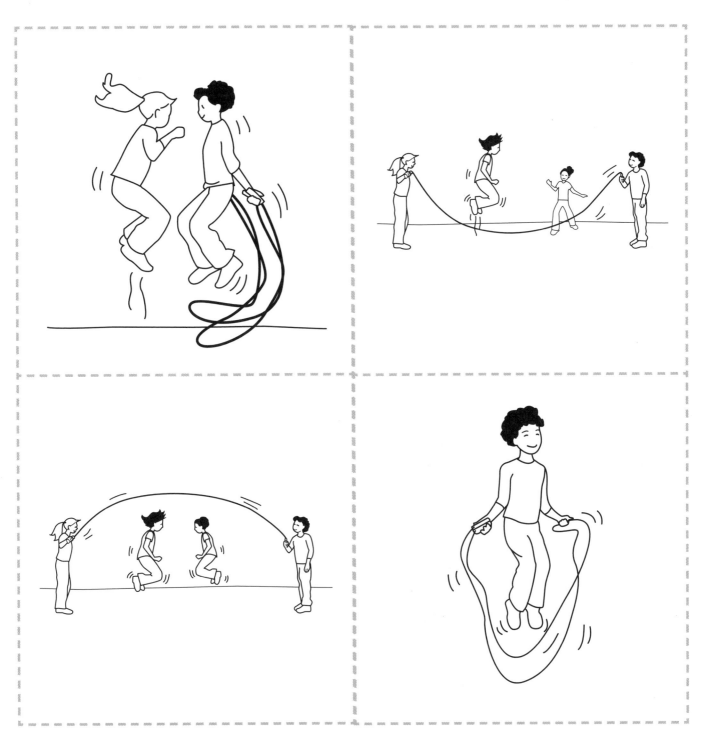

**Cut out the pictures. Put them in the correct order.
Then glue them onto another sheet of paper.**

The Parade

Read the story.

"How was the parade?" asked Gramma.

"It was great!" said Sara.

"First, the floats came by. I liked the ones with lots of flowers.

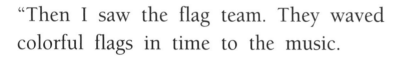

"Next was the marching band. The music they played made me feel like marching along.

"Then I saw the flag team. They waved colorful flags in time to the music.

"Finally, I saw the clowns. They made me laugh. They were throwing candy, too!"

"I love parades!" said Gramma. "I wish I could have gone."

"That's why I'm here!" said Sara. "I brought you some candy. I took pictures, too. Let's load them on your computer right now!"

Draw lines to answer the questions.

What did Sara see first in the parade?	**marching band**
What did Sara see next?	**Gramma**
What did Sara see then?	**clowns**
What did Sara see last?	**flag team**
Who did Sara see after the parade?	**floats**

Snow!

Read the story. Number the pictures to show the right order.

Jake woke up and looked out the window. Snow!
"I'm going sledding!" he shouted.

"First, you must have breakfast," said Mom.

Jake ate some bacon, eggs, and toast.

"Next, you must put on warm clothes," said Mom.

Jake put on a coat, boots, gloves, and a stocking cap.

"Now, you must find your sled," said Mom.

Jake looked in the shed and garage.

Then he went to the basement. He was there a long time.

"Finally!" he said, spotting the sled in the back of a closet.

Jake went outside. The snow had melted!

"At least you'll be ready for the next snow," said Mom.

Assessment

Read the story. Then record the events in order on the graphic organizer.

"I'm going to help Dad with the Saturday chores," Monica thought.

"First, I'll clean my room."

After breakfast, Monica said, "I'll wash the dishes, Dad!"

When she was done, she went outside.

While Dad mowed the lawn, she raked the clippings into neat piles.

Dad and Monica went inside. Monica made lunch.

Then she helped Dad dust and vacuum the living room.

"I'm tired!" Monica said.

"Me, too!" said Dad. "But I got the chores done a lot faster with your help, so we can play some games now. How does that sound?"

"Great!" said Monica. "I'm going to help every Saturday!"

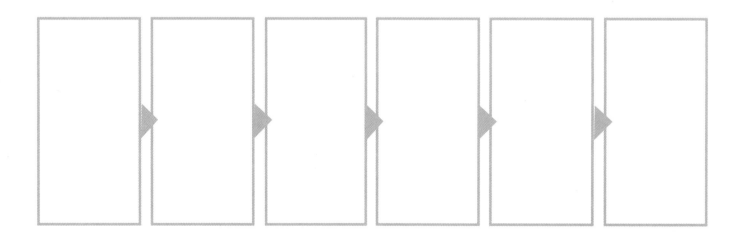

Overview Identify Sequence of Events in Nonfiction

Directions and Sample Answers for Activity Pages

Day 1	See "Provide a Real-World Example" below.
Day 2	Discuss the pictures. Then ask students to cut out the pictures, put them in the correct order, and glue them onto another sheet of paper. (making cards, walking outside, delivering cards, patient opening card)
Day 3	Discuss the pictures. Then ask students to number the sentences in the correct order. (4, 1, 5, 3, 2)
Day 4	Read and discuss the passage. Then help students number the sentences in the correct order. (7, 3, 4, 1, 6, 5, 2)
Day 5	Read the passage together. Ask students to fill in the graphic organizer. Afterward, meet individually with students to discuss their results. Use their responses to plan further instruction and review. (built a huge wooden slide, poured cold water on the slide, water froze, sleds raced down the icy slide)

Provide a Real-World Example

◆ Hand out the Day 1 activity page.

◆ **Say:** *Once I watched two men repair the sidewalk on my street. First, they unloaded their truck. Next, they put all their tools on the grass. Then they talked about what they needed to do. Finally, they got started on their work. Doing things in a certain order is called a sequence of events.*

◆ Ask students to write the number 1 on the picture that shows what the men did first. Ask them to write the number 2 on the picture that shows what happened next. Ask them to write the number 3 on the picture that shows what the men did then. Ask them to write the number 4 on the picture that shows what the men did last.

◆ Ask students to use the empty squares to draw their own sequence of events and share it with partners.

◆ Explain that they can also find a sequence of events when they read. Write the following on chart paper:

Identifying Sequence of Events in Nonfiction

Find evidence in the pictures.

Find words that tell about order, such as *first, next, then, now, after,* and *finally.*

Think about the order in which things usually happen.

At Work

Listen. Then number each picture in the correct order.

Now draw your own sequence of events below.

Special Delivery

Read the passage.

Many classes do community service projects. One project is making cards. Your class can make cards for people in hospitals or nursing homes. These cards cheer people up and let them know that someone cares.

Cut out the pictures. Put them in the correct order.
Then glue them onto another sheet of paper.

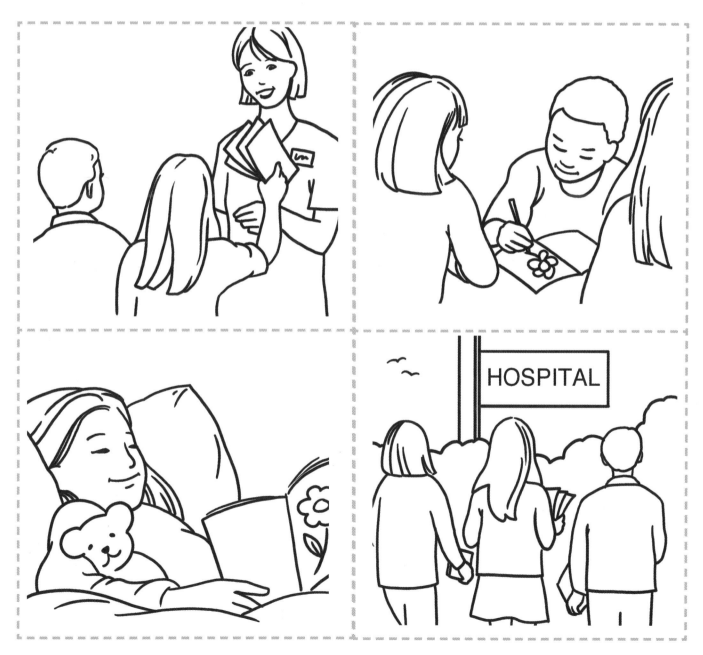

Laundry Day

Many kids help with the laundry at home. Follow these steps:

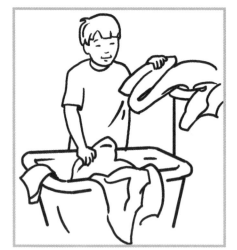  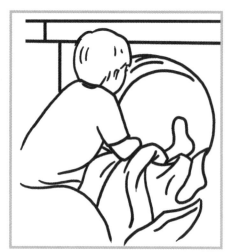

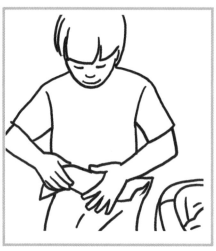 

Number the sentences in the correct order.

_____ Put the dirty clothes in the washing machine.

_____ Put the folded clothes away.

_____ Fold the clean, dry clothes.

_____ Get the dirty clothes.

_____ Put the clean clothes in the dryer.

Old Paper, New Paper

Read the passage.

Do you recycle old paper? You should!

Old paper can become new paper.

After you take your old paper to a recycling center, truckers deliver it to a mill.

First, a machine chops up the paper.

Then another machine mixes the paper with hot water.

Next, a third machine cleans the paper.

Now, the old paper is pulp.

People use the pulp to make new paper.

Number the sentences in the correct order.

_____ A machine mixes the paper with hot water.

_____ People make new paper with the pulp.

_____ Truckers deliver the paper to a mill.

_____ A machine chops up the paper.

_____ The paper becomes pulp.

_____ A machine cleans the paper.

_____ People take old paper to a recycling center.

Assessment

Read the passage. Then record the events in order on the graphic organizer.

Do you like to ride roller coasters?

Up . . . down . . . looping around . . . what a ride!

Hundreds of years ago, some clever people invented the first roller coaster.

First, they built a huge wooden slide.

Then they poured cold water on the slide.

Since it was winter, the water froze.

Large sleds raced down the icy slide . . . what a ride!

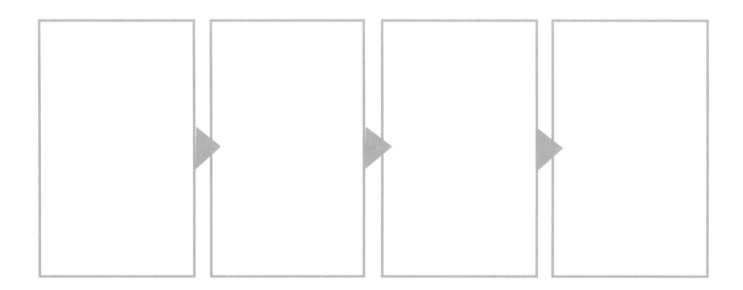

Overview Analyzing Story Elements: Setting

Directions and Sample Answers for Activity Pages

Day 1	See "Provide a Real-World Example" below.
Day 2	Discuss each picture. Then ask students to identify and label the pictures that show a setting. (library, bedroom, soccer field, desert, spaceship)
Day 3	Read and discuss each phrase. Help students identify and circle the phrases that tell about settings. Then help students write a phrase about a setting. (a stormy night, a messy kitchen, the top of a tall building, a computer store, early the next morning, a candy shop)
Day 4	Read and discuss each passage. Then help students underline the setting clues and write when and where each story takes place. (**Clues:** woke up, sun, books, stuffed animals, desk, backpack. **Setting:** morning in a girl's bedroom. **Clues:** colorful fallen leaves, deer, trees, squirrels, branches. **Setting:** a forest in the autumn. **Clues:** large door, first floor, crowded and noisy, smelled of perfume, Monday Moonlight Sale, escalator. **Setting:** Monday night in a large department store.)
Day 5	Read the passage together. Ask students to record the setting clues and setting on their graphic organizers. Afterward, meet individually with students to discuss their results. Use their responses to plan further instruction and review. (**Clues:** place is huge, other classes here, map, dinosaur exhibit, planet exhibit, cafeteria, gift shop, whole day ahead of us. **Setting:** morning in a science museum.)

Provide a Real-World Example

◆ Hand out the Day 1 activity page.

◆ **Say:** *Today we will talk about setting. A setting is when and where something takes place. We are in a setting right now. I see the time on the clock. The time is a clue. I see clues in the room, too. I see my desk and the reading corner. I see books. I see you! These clues tell me that our setting is daytime in a classroom.*

◆ Invite students to look at the pictures and describe the settings they see. With a partner, invite them to tell a story that could happen in one of these settings.

◆ **Ask:** *What other settings can you think of? Remember that the place can be real or imaginary. The time can be now, in the past, or in the future.*

◆ Explain that they can also analyze settings when they read stories. Write the following on chart paper:

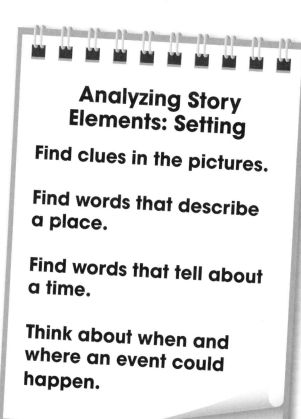

Analyzing Story Elements: Setting

Find clues in the pictures.

Find words that describe a place.

Find words that tell about a time.

Think about when and where an event could happen.

What Might Happen?

Choose a setting. Then tell a story that might happen in that setting.

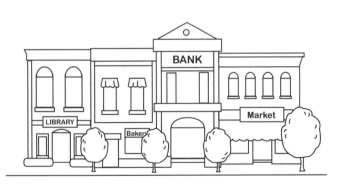

Name a Setting

Look at the pictures. Label the pictures that show a setting.

| spaceship | desert | soccer field | pumpkin |
| woman | library | frame | bedroom |

_____   _____   _____   _____

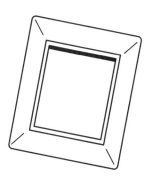

_____   _____   _____   _____

Circle a Setting

Read the phrases. Draw a circle around each phrase that tells about a setting.

a stormy night

running late

a messy kitchen

a computer store

my favorite uncle

an unhappy pup

the top of a tall building

early the next morning

my brothers and sisters

a candy shop

Write another phrase that tells about a setting.

_____

Setting Clues

**Read each passage. Draw a line under the setting clues.
Then write when and where the story takes place.**

Emma woke up. The sun shone through the window.

Emma saw her books, stuffed animals, and desk.

She saw her backpack all ready for school.

This story takes place _____

in a _____ .

Tony and Jeff crunched through the colorful fallen
leaves.

A deer ran in front of them, dodging the trees.

Frightened squirrels ran along the branches.

This story takes place _____

in a _____ .

Kelly and Mom pushed open the large door.

The first floor was crowded and noisy. It smelled of
perfume.

"Welcome to the Monday Moonlight Sale," a woman
said.

"Thank you!" replied Mom as they headed for the
escalator.

This story takes place _____

in a _____ .

Assessment

Read the story. Write the clues. Then name the setting.

"Wow!" said Mia. "This place is huge! And look at all the other classes here, too!"

Mr. Norr picked up a map.

"Let's see the dinosaur exhibit first," he said.

"Then can we go to the aerospace room?" asked Anna. "I want to see the planet exhibit."

"We should have time to visit both before eating lunch in the cafeteria," Mr. Norr replied. "Then we'll check out the other exhibits."

"Can we stop by the gift shop before we leave?" asked Grant.

"We'll try to do everything," Mr. Norr said. "We have the whole day ahead of us!"

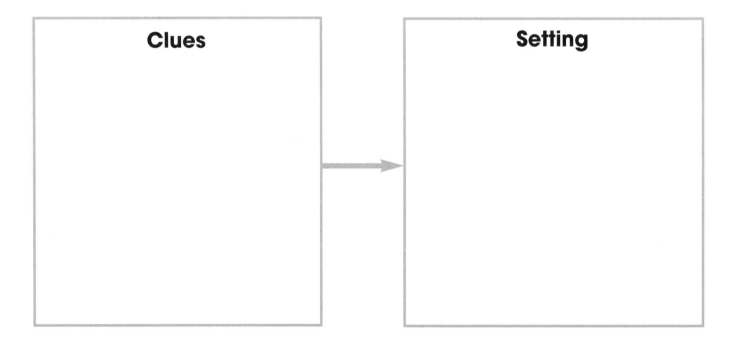

Clues	Setting

Overview   Analyzing Story Elements: Plot

Directions and Sample Answers for Activity Pages

Day 1	See "Provide a Real-World Example" below.
Day 2	Discuss the pictures. Then ask students to identify the picture that shows the beginning of each plot and write the story problem on the line. (A box falls from a truck. A girl is hungry. A boy is sad.)
Day 3	Discuss the pictures. Then ask students to draw or write what might happen in the middle of each plot. (Responses will vary.)
Day 4	Read the beginning and middle of the story together. Discuss. Then ask students to write an ending. (Responses will vary.)
Day 5	Read the story together. Ask students to write what happened at the beginning, middle, and end of the story. Afterward, meet individually with students to discuss their results. Use their responses to plan further instruction and review. (**Beginning:** Merry doesn't want her baby brother to play in her room. **Middle:** Merry finds toys for Brett to play with. **End:** Brett, Mom, and Merry all feel better.)

Provide a Real-World Example

◆ Hand out the Day 1 activity page.

◆ **Say:** *Imagine that four friends are ready for a picnic. Suddenly, they realize they have forgotten to bring forks. What will they do? Sherea lives the closest, so she offers to go back home for forks. The others wait. Soon, Sherea comes back and they are off to the picnic, late but happy.*

◆ Ask students to Think/Pair/Share other things the kids could have done. Then **say:** *These events are like the plot of a story. The beginning of the story tells a problem. The middle of the story tells what the characters do. The end of the story tells the solution to the problem.*

◆ Write the words **beginning**, **middle**, and **end** on the board. Ask students to look at the top row of pictures and write the correct word under each picture. Then discuss the pictures on the next two rows and help students label the story parts.

◆ Explain that they can also analyze plots when they read stories. Write the following on chart paper:

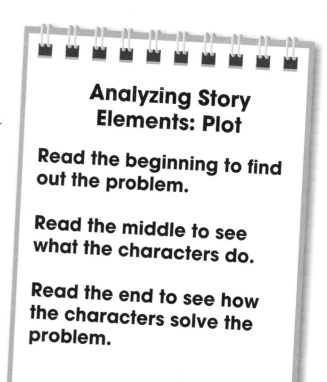

Analyzing Story Elements: Plot

Read the beginning to find out the problem.

Read the middle to see what the characters do.

Read the end to see how the characters solve the problem.

Stories

Look at each row of pictures. Then write *beginning*, *middle*, or *end* below each picture.

_____ _____ _____

_____ _____ _____

_____ _____ _____

Name _____

Start the Story

**Find the picture that shows the beginning of each plot.
Write the story problem on the line.**

Story Problem: _____

_____

Story Problem: _____

_____

Story Problem: _____

_____

Name _____

In the Middle

Look at the pictures. Draw or write what might happen in the middle of each plot.

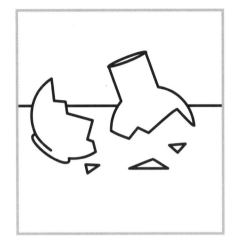

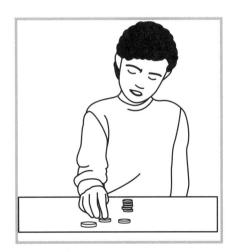

The Swim Meet

**Read the beginning and middle of the plot.
Then write an ending.**

Beginning

Jake sighed. "I haven't won a single swim medal this summer," he complained.

"Hmm . . ." said Jake's big sister Selma.

"You're lucky—you've won lots of swim medals," said Jake. "It's not fair!"

Selma laughed. "You left out one small detail," she said. "I practice every day. You should try it!"

Middle

Jake thought about what Selma had said. Selma DID practice every day, even on weekends. Maybe "lucky" or "fair" didn't have anything to do with her collection of medals.

"Selma, could I start going to the pool with you?" Jake asked. "I want to get ready for next week's swim meet."

"Sure!" said Selma. "Let's go right now!"

End

_____

_____

_____

Name _____

Assessment

Read the story. Then write what happened at the beginning, middle, and end of the story.

"Mom! Brett's in my room again!" shouted Merry.

Mom came to the door. "He's just a little boy," Mom said. "He can't be that much of a bother."

"Why do I have to be the only girl in third grade with a pesky baby brother?" Merry asked.

Suddenly, Merry had an idea. She emptied the bottom two shelves of her bookcase. Then she dug through her closet and found her old toys to put on the shelves. "These are for you," she said to Brett.

Brett gave Merry a hug. Mom smiled. "He IS kind of cute," Merry admitted.

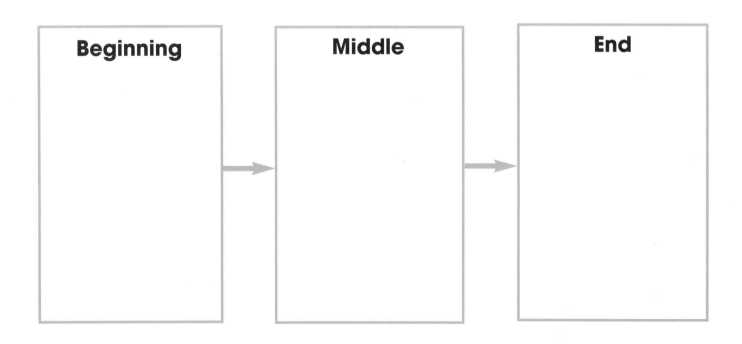

Beginning	**Middle**	**End**

Overview Analyzing Character: Traits

Directions and Sample Answers for Activity Pages

Day 1	See "Provide a Real-World Example" below.
Day 2	Ask students to think about someone they know well and someone who would make a good friend. Then ask them to complete the sentences to describe these people's traits. Remind them that the sentences should provide clues about the traits. (**Example:** My uncle is friendly because he always smiles and waves at people. Good friends are caring. They call you when you're sick.)
Day 3	Read and discuss the story. Then ask students to circle Samantha's traits and write a clue for one of the traits. (**Traits:** energetic, stubborn, fair. **Clue for "fair":** Samantha agreed to Rashib's compromise.)
Day 4	Read about Tweet and Lucky. Discuss. Then ask students to circle the best answer to each question and explain their answers. (**Friendly:** Tweet—talks to Mandy. **Athletic:** Lucky—runs on his wheel. **Noisy:** Tweet—only quiets down when Mandy puts a sheet over her cage. **Quiet:** Lucky—doesn't pay much attention to Mandy.)
Day 5	Read the passage together. Ask students to write clues about Aunt Lu and name one of her traits on their graphic organizers. Afterward, meet individually with students to discuss their results. Use their responses to plan further instruction and review. (**Clues:** takes time with her students and helps them when they're having trouble. **Trait:** kind.)

Provide a Real-World Example

◆ Hand out the Day 1 activity page.

◆ **Say:** *You are different from the person sitting near you. That is because every person has certain traits, or special features. Being cheerful is a trait. So is being shy. Traits show up in the things we think, do, and say.*

◆ Together, read and discuss each trait on the page. Then invite students to put a check mark in front of the traits that describe themselves.

◆ **Say:** *Think of a character in a movie you have watched. Put a check mark in front of the traits that tell about the character. Do you share some of the same traits?*

◆ Explain that students can also analyze character traits when they read stories. Write the following on chart paper:

Analyzing Character: Traits

Find clues in the pictures.

Find clues in the words.

Think about what the character thinks, says, and does.

Think of words that describe the character.

Name _____

The Two of You

Describe yourself. Then describe a movie character.

Me

____ cheerful

____ shy

____ kind

____ bossy

____ patient

____ friendly

____ clever

____ quiet

____ fair

____ lively

____ witty

____ trustworthy

Name of Movie:

_____

Name of Character:

_____

____ cheerful

____ shy

____ kind

____ bossy

____ patient

____ friendly

____ clever

____ quiet

____ fair

____ lively

____ witty

____ trustworthy

Unit 7 • Everyday Comprehension Intervention Activities Grade 3 • ©2010 Newmark Learning, LLC

Traits

Think about someone you know well. Write three sentences about the person's traits.

_____ is _____ because

_____.

_____ is _____ because

_____.

_____ is _____ because

_____.

**Think about the traits you look for in a good friend.
Write three sentences about these traits.**

Good friends are _____.

They _____.

Good friends are _____.

They _____.

Good friends are _____.

They _____.

At the Pond

Read the story.

"Let's swim at the pond today," said Samantha. "We can run all the way there."

"I don't want to run and swim," said Rashib. "I want to play a card game at home."

"Well, I don't want to play cards. I like to get exercise!" Samantha insisted.

She and Rashib stared at each other with their arms crossed over their chests.

"Let's compromise," Rashib finally said. "Let's walk to the pond. First, we can swim. Then we can play cards on the grass."

Samantha hugged her brother. "That's a great idea!" she shouted. "Let's go!"

Draw a circle around Samantha's traits.

energetic   shy   bossy

patient   stubborn   fair

Write a clue for one of Samantha's traits.

Trait:_____

Clue:_____

Mandy's Pets

Read about two pets.

Mandy has two pets—a bird named Tweet and a hamster named Lucky.

"Hi, Mandy," Tweet says when Mandy comes into the room.

"Bye, Mandy," she says when Mandy leaves the room.

"Good night, Tweet!" Mandy says as she puts a sheet over Tweet's cage each evening.

It's the only way to make Tweet quiet down!

Lucky lives in a cage, too. He likes to run on his wheel.

He doesn't pay much attention to Mandy when she tries to play with him.

He does pay attention to his hamster snacks, though!

Circle the best answer. Then tell how you know.

Which pet would you say is **friendly**?   Tweet   Lucky

Why? _____

Which pet would you say is **athletic**?   Tweet   Lucky

Why? _____

Which pet would you say is **noisy**?   Tweet   Lucky

Why?_____

Which pet would you say is **quiet**?   Tweet   Lucky

Why? _____

Assessment

Read the diary entry. Then write clues about Aunt Lu and name one of her traits.

Dear Diary,

Have I told you about my Aunt Lu?

On Saturdays, she teaches painting.

Her students love her because she takes time with them. She helps them when they're having trouble.

Sometimes her paintings are in a show.

People even buy her paintings!

Aunt Lu didn't have class today, so we spent the whole day together.

She always wants to do what I want to do.

This time, we went ice skating and had hot chocolate.

Aunt Lu is totally my favorite aunt.

I can't wait for her to visit again!

    Your friend,

    Karinda

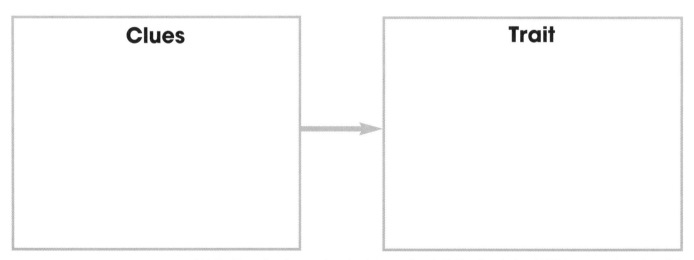

Clues	→	**Trait**

Overview Analyzing Character: Feelings

Directions and Sample Answers for Activity Pages

Day 1	See "Provide a Real-World Example" below.
Day 2	Discuss each picture. Then ask students to complete the sentence to describe how the person feels. (excited/his team scored; nervous/she is at the dentist; scared/the alligator looks mean; happy/she receives a gift)
Day 3	Read and discuss the story. Then ask students to answer the questions about Grace. (**At first:** puzzled/She was not sure what to do. **At the end:** proud/She made Mom happy.)
Day 4	Read and discuss the story. Then ask students to complete the sentences and write a clue for each feeling. (**Tony:** nervous/the biggest test of the year. **Janey:** confident/studied hard. **Kendra:** tired/could hardly stay awake, stayed up late.)
Day 5	Read the passage together. Ask students to write clues about Cassie and tell how she feels on their graphic organizers. Afterward, meet individually with students to discuss their results. Use their responses to plan further instruction and review. (**Clues:** spent the whole day in the park, ran races, played games, had a picnic, teachers played, really cool, said good-bye to friends, almost cried, miss them. **Feelings:** excited, sad.)

Provide a Real-World Example

◆ Hand out the Day 1 activity page.

◆ **Say:** *We all have different feelings at different times. I remember a day I moved to a new community. I had many different feelings! I was excited about living there, but I was uneasy because I didn't know my way around yet.*

◆ Together, read and discuss each feeling on the page. Then ask students to think about a time they made a big move or started something new. Invite them to put a check mark in front of the feelings they had that day.

◆ **Ask:** *What about the other people in your family? How do you think they felt that day? Put a check mark in front of the feelings they had. Did you share some of the same feelings?*

◆ Explain that students can also analyze a character's feelings when they read stories. Write the following on chart paper:

Analyzing Character: Feelings

Find clues in the pictures.

Find clues in the words.

Think about what the character thinks, says, and does.

Think of words that describe how the character feels.

A Big Change

Think of a time when you made a big move or started something new. Describe how you felt that day. Then describe how a family member felt that day.

Me	**Family Member**
_____ excited	_____ excited
_____ uneasy	_____ uneasy
_____ eager	_____ eager
_____ calm	_____ calm
_____ worried	_____ worried
_____ lonely	_____ lonely
_____ brave	_____ brave
_____ happy	_____ happy
_____ angry	_____ angry
_____ proud	_____ proud
_____ puzzled	_____ puzzled
_____ lost	_____ lost

How Do They Feel?

Look at each picture. Then complete the sentence.

He feels _____ because

_____ .

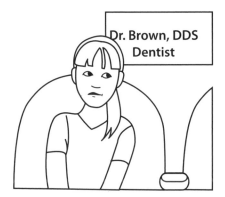

She feels _____ because

_____ .

He feels _____ because

_____ .

She feels _____ because

_____ .

A Special Day

Read the story.

"Since today is your day off, can we do something special?" asked Grace.

"Sure!" said Mom. "Would you like to go roller skating or bike riding? I know you like both those things."

Grace thought about Mom's suggestions. She did like roller skating and bike riding.

But Mom wasn't very good at roller skating. She liked to spend time at the library.

"I know!" said Grace. "Let's ride our bikes to the library!"

"Great plan!" said Mom. "I love spending my days off with you!"

Draw a circle around the best answers. Then answer the questions.

How did Grace feel at first?   **puzzled**   **sad**

How do you know? _____

_____

How do you think Grace felt at the end?   **brave**   **proud**

Why? _____

_____

The Big Test

Read the story.

Tony sat up straight.
He lined up his pencils and checked his eraser.

"This is it," he thought. "The biggest test of
the year."

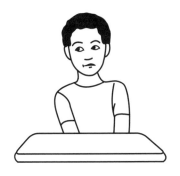

Janey was at the desk next to Tony.

She smiled and sat back in her chair.

"I'm glad I studied so hard this year!" she
thought.

Kendra slumped in her chair in the back
of the room.

She could hardly stay awake.

"I don't think staying up late was a good
idea," she thought.

Complete the sentences.
Then write a clue to tell how you know.

I think Tony feels _____.

Clue:_____

I think Janey feels _____.

Clue:_____

I think Kendra feels _____.

Clue:_____

Assessment

**Read the diary entry. Write clues about Cassie.
Then tell how she feels.**

Dear Diary,

Today was the last day of school.

We spent the whole day outside in the park.

We ran races, played games, and had a picnic.

Our teachers played with us. It was really cool!

At the end of the day, I said good-bye to my friends.

I almost started to cry. I'll miss them so much!

We're going to e-mail in the summer.

I hope they can come visit me, too.

     Cassie

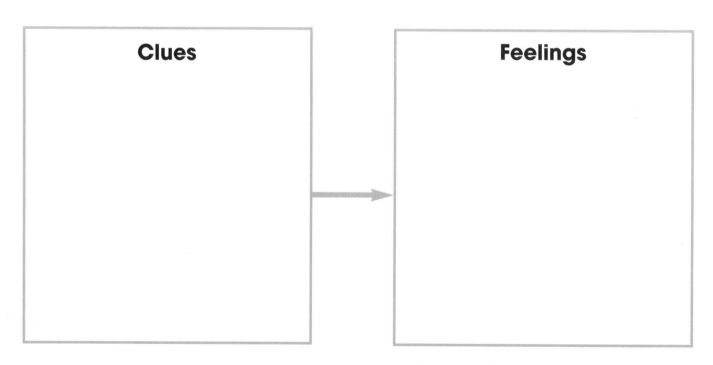

Clues	**Feelings**

Overview Identifying Stated Main Idea

Directions and Sample Answers for Activity Pages

Day 1	See "Provide a Real-World Example" below.
Day 2	Read and discuss the passage. Then ask students to draw a line under the stated main idea in each paragraph. (A star is a giant ball of hot gas. The sun is our closest star. The North Star helps people find their way at night. A moon is not a star.)
Day 3	Read and discuss the passage. Ask students to locate and color the stated main idea, the sentence that doesn't belong, and the new tree. (**1:** A single tree can create a forest. **2:** Trees make shade for people to enjoy. **3:** See illustration.)
Day 4	Read and discuss the passage. Then ask students to answer the questions. (**1:** the Wright brothers. **2:** Two brothers invented the airplane. **3:** Responses will vary.)
Day 5	Read the passage together. Ask students to read the supporting details in the second box on the graphic organizer. Then ask them to look back at the passage, find the stated main idea, and write it in the first box. Afterward, meet individually with students to discuss their results. Use their responses to plan further instruction and review. (**Stated main idea:** Some termites build tall towers to live in.)

Provide a Real-World Example

◆ Hand out the Day 1 activity page.

◆ **Say:** *I heard someone speak about quilt collecting the other day. The speaker showed several colorful quilts she had found at flea markets. Many of them were quite old. The woman stated that collecting quilts is a fun and interesting hobby.*

◆ Help students complete the main idea that the woman stated about collecting quilts. Then ask them to draw a picture of something else people collect and complete a main idea statement about that collection.

◆ Explain that students can also identify stated main ideas when they read. Write the following on chart paper:

Identifying Stated Main Idea

See what the passage is about.

Find details about the topic.

Find the sentence that tells about the details.

Find the sentence that tells the most important idea.

Collecting

Listen. Then complete the stated main idea.

Stated Main Idea:

Collecting quilts is a _____ hobby.

Draw something else that people collect.
Write a main idea statement about what you've drawn.

```



```

Main Idea Statement:

_____.

Stars

Read the passage. Draw a line under the stated main idea in each paragraph.

What is a star?

People used to think it was simply a tiny light in the night sky.

Now we know that a star is a giant ball of hot gas.

The sun is our closest star.

It looks bigger than all the other stars.

It only looks bigger because it is so close.

Have you heard of the North Star, or Polaris?

It is in a group of stars called the Little Dipper.

The North Star helps people find their way at night.

A moon is not a star.

One moon orbits around Earth.

Earth's moon is a ball of gray rock and dust.

How Does a Forest Grow?

Read the passage.

How does a forest grow?

A single tree can create a forest!

First, the tree produces seeds.

Then the seeds fall on the soil.

Leaves fall and make the soil better.

The leaves protect the tiny seeds, too.

Rain waters the seeds.

Soon, a tiny tree begins to sprout.

When the tree grows up, it makes more seeds.

More trees start to grow.

Trees make shade for people to enjoy.

Soon, Earth has a new forest!

1. Find the stated main idea. Color it red.

2. Find a sentence that does not belong. Color it blue.

3. Find the new tree in the picture. Color it green.

The Wright Brothers

Read the passage. Then answer the questions.

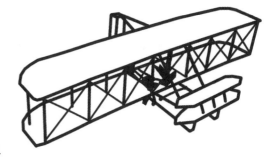

Did you know that two brothers invented the airplane?

Orville and Wilbur Wright wanted to find a way for people to fly.

First, they made a glider. It flew like a kite, but it was hard to steer.

Next, they added wings. This new glider flew for a very short distance.

Then they tried something new. They added a motor.

In 1903, the Wright brothers flew the very first airplane!

1. Who is the passage about? _____

2. What is the stated main idea?

   _____

3. What else would you like to learn about the first airplanes?

   _____

   _____

Assessment

**Read the passage. Read the supporting details on the graphic organizer.
Then write the stated main idea.**

Have you ever heard of an insect whose home is a tower? Some termites build tall towers to live in. They make the towers out of mud. These towers can be more that 20 feet (6 meters) high—taller than many human buildings! The towers shelter the termites from rain, storms, and wind. The towers are also a good place for termites to hide when danger is near.

Stated Main Idea

↓

Supporting Details

Overview Identifying Supporting Details

Directions and Sample Answers for Activity Pages

Day 1	See "Provide a Real-World Example" below.
Day 2	Read the passages together. Discuss the stated main ideas. Then ask students to circle the supporting details in each passage. (**First:** stalactites hang from the roof, stalagmites form on the bottom. **Second:** sail over the land, do not use fuel, simply float in the air. **Third:** work together to pass laws to stop pollution, remove trash from parks and beaches, recycle paper and cans.)
Day 3	Read and discuss each paragraph and stated main idea. Then ask students to write details that support each main idea. (**First:** hot, dry, not enough water, temperature can reach over 110° Fahrenheit (over 43° Celsius). **Second:** not hot, covered with pebbles and large rocks. **Third:** Arctic and Antarctic regions of Earth, no liquid water.)
Day 4	Read and discuss each paragraph and stated main idea. Then ask students to locate and color the circle in front of each supporting detail from the paragraph. (**First:** have webbed feet, can walk, have wings that help them swim, are birds. **Second:** krill are shrimp, eat fish under the water, have a favorite food, krill are small.)
Day 5	Read the passage together. Ask students to write the stated main idea in the first box on the graphic organizer. Then ask them to write the supporting details in the second box. Afterward, meet individually with students to discuss their results. Use their responses to plan further instruction and review. (**Stated Main Idea:** The long journey west was hard for settlers. **Supporting Details:** carried all their belongings in covered wagons, drove through rivers and over mountains, sun beat down on them, dealt with freezing wind and snow.)

Provide a Real-World Example

◆ Hand out the Day 1 activity page.

◆ **Say:** My friend works in a pet store. She loves her job and talks about it often. She stated that there are many things to see and do in a pet store. What are some details she might share about her job?

◆ Allow time for students to respond. Then ask them to complete the stated main idea on their page, draw a circle around the pictures that show things you can see or do in a pet store, and draw or write about one other thing you might see or do there. **Say:** These different sights and activities are details. The details support the main idea stated on the page.

◆ Explain that students can also identify supporting details when they read. Write the following on chart paper:

Identifying Supporting Details

See what the passage is about.

Find the sentence that tells the most important idea.

Find sentences that tell more information about the main idea.

Pet Store

Listen. Circle the supporting details. Then complete the stated main idea.

Stated Main Idea:

There are many things to _____ in a pet store.

What else might you see in a pet store? Draw or write your ideas below.

Our Earth

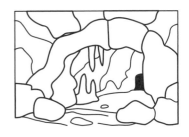

Read the passages.

Exploring Earth's caves can be fun.

You can see amazing rock shapes in a cave.

Some rocks, such as stalactites, hang from the roof of the cave.

Other rocks, such as stalagmites, form on the bottom of the cave.

Stated Main Idea: You can see amazing rock shapes in a cave.

Circle the details that tell more about the main idea.

How would you like to sail over the land?

You can do that in a sailplane.

Sailplanes are a way to explore Earth without harming it.

They do not use fuel—they simply float in the air.

Stated Main Idea: Sailplanes are a way to explore Earth without harming it.

Circle the details that tell more about the main idea.

There are many ways to take care of Earth.

We can work together to pass laws to stop pollution.

We can remove our trash from parks and beaches.

We can recycle paper and cans.

Stated Main Idea: There are many ways to take care of Earth.

Circle the details that tell more about the main idea.

Deserts

Read each paragraph. Read the stated main idea. Then write details that support each main idea.

Most deserts are hot, dry places. It is hard for many animals, plants, and people to survive in a hot desert.

There is not enough water, and the temperature can reach over 110° Fahrenheit (over 43° Celsius).

Stated Main Idea: It is hard for many animals, plants, and people to survive in a desert.

Supporting Details: _____

_____

Not all deserts are hot. Some deserts are in cooler areas of Earth. Many of these deserts are covered with pebbles and large rocks.

Stated Main Idea: Some deserts are in cooler areas of Earth.

Supporting Details: _____

_____

The Arctic and Antarctic regions of Earth have polar deserts. Polar deserts are cold and icy. They are still deserts because there is no liquid water.

Stated Main Idea: Polar deserts are cold and icy.

Supporting Details: _____

_____

Penguins

Read each paragraph. Find the underlined stated main idea. Then color in the circle in front of each supporting detail you read in the paragraph.

Penguins are birds, but they are swimming birds. <u>Penguins are very good swimmers</u>. They have wings that help them swim. They have webbed feet that help them swim, too. They can stand and walk on their feet.

○ have webbed feet

○ have fur to keep warm

○ can walk

○ have wings that help them swim

○ swim everywhere they go

○ are birds

<u>Penguins dive under the water to get food.</u> They eat fish when they are under the water. Their favorite food to eat underwater is krill. Krill are small shrimp.

○ krill are shrimp

○ catch fish to drag to their nests

○ eat fish under the water

○ have a favorite food

○ krill are small

○ do not eat shrimp

Name _____

Assessment

Read the passage. Write the stated main idea in the first box. Then write the supporting details.

In the 1700s, people in the United States began to move west to find land on which to settle. The long journey west was hard for settlers. They packed all their belongings in covered wagons. Then they drove these wagons through rivers and over mountains. The blazing heat of the sun beat down on them in summer. In winter, they dealt with freezing wind and snow.

Stated Main Idea	Supporting Details

Overview Summarizing Fiction

Directions and Sample Answers for Activity Pages

Day 1	See "Provide a Real-World Example" below.
Day 2	Discuss the pictures. Ask students to tell the story to a partner. Then ask them to select and circle the best summary. (A family tries to find a lost shoe, but the dog has it all along.)
Day 3	Read and discuss the story. Ask students to underline the big ideas and complete the sentence to write a summary. (**Big Ideas:** two small fish, saw a giant fish, hid behind a rock, were safe. **Summary:** Two small fish stay safe by hiding from a big fish.)
Day 4	Read and discuss the story. Ask students to underline the big idea and write a summary of the story. (**Big Ideas:** wish today was someone's birthday, celebrating birthdays all over the world, have a party for them, bake a cake, bring juice, put up paper streamers. **Summary:** Three kids have a party to celebrate birthdays around the world.)
Day 5	Read the story together. Ask students to write the big ideas and summary on their graphic organizers. Afterward, meet individually with students to discuss their results. Use their responses to plan further instruction and review. (**Big Ideas:** big, very big, weighed 100 pounds at two weeks old, put cradle in ocean, rock him to sleep, huge waves crashed onto coasts and islands. **Summary:** Paul Bunyan was so big that his rocking cradle created huge waves in the ocean.)

Provide a Real-World Example

◆ Hand out the Day 1 activity page.

◆ **Say:** *Many people enjoy going to the library. What are some things people do at the library?* Allow time for students to respond, and then **say:** *I can tell about the library in one sentence:* **People read, use computers, and learn new things at the library.** *This sentence is a summary of things people do there.*

◆ Pair students and ask them to summarize a trip to a place they enjoy.

◆ Then ask students to look at the pictures on the activity page and summarize the story. If they have difficulty, offer some suggestions, such as *A boy helped his mom take care of the new baby.*

◆ Explain that they can also summarize stories they read. Write the following on chart paper:

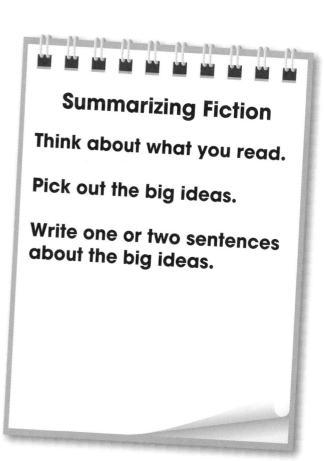

Summarizing Fiction

Think about what you read.

Pick out the big ideas.

Write one or two sentences about the big ideas.

New Baby

Look at the pictures. Then summarize the story.

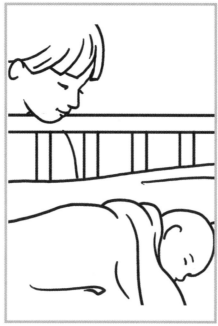

Unit 11 • Everyday Comprehension Intervention Activities Grade 3 • ©2010 Newmark Learning, LLC

Lost Shoe

Look at the pictures. Tell the story to a partner.

 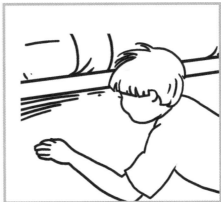 

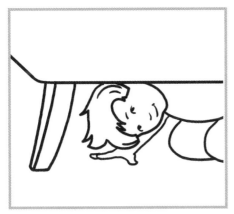  

Draw a circle around the best summary.

A family has breakfast together and then looks for the dog.

A boy lost his shoe, so he cannot go to school that day.

A family tries to find a lost shoe, but the dog has it all along.

Fish Tag

Read the story. Draw a line under the big ideas.

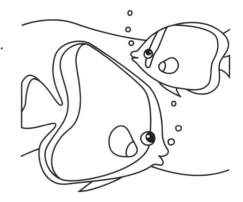

Two small fish, Fig and Swish, lived in the ocean. They saw each other every day.

"Do you want to play tag?" Fig asked Swish.

"Sure!" said Swish. "You're it!" Swish swam away as fast as he could.

Suddenly, Fig saw a giant fish swimming after Swish. "Hide, Swish!" he called.

Swish hid behind a rock and beckoned Fig to join him.

A few minutes later, Fig peeked out. "He's gone—we're safe!" he said.

"That was a close one!" said Swish.

"We didn't get to play tag, did we?" asked Fig.

"No . . . but we got to play hide-and-seek!" replied Swish with a laugh.

Complete the sentence to write a summary.

Two _____ stay _____

by _____.

Happy Birthday!

Read the story. Draw a line under the big ideas.

"I wish today was someone's birthday," said Anne. "Then we could have a party."

"It is SOMEONE'S birthday," said Pam. "People are celebrating birthdays all over the world today."

"Well, let's have a party for them," said Mike. "My sister will help us bake a cake."

"I can bring juice," said Anne.

"I can put up paper streamers," said Pam.

Everyone got busy, and soon they were ready to cut the cake.

"Happy birthday around the world!" said Anne.

"Happy birthday around the word!" echoed Pam and Mike.

Write a summary of the story.

_____

_____

_____

_____

Assessment

**Read the tall tale. Write the big ideas.
Then write a summary.**

Paul Bunyan was big. In fact, he was VERY big.

"My, what a big baby we have," said his mother. "He's only two weeks old, and he already weighs 100 pounds!"

When Paul cried, his parents didn't know what to do. "Let's put his cradle in the ocean," they said. "We can rock him to sleep." So that is what they did. But their plan didn't work out so well. Every time that cradle rocked, huge waves crashed onto all the ocean's coasts and islands.

"Our Paul is going to lead an interesting life," sighed Paul's mother. And he did.

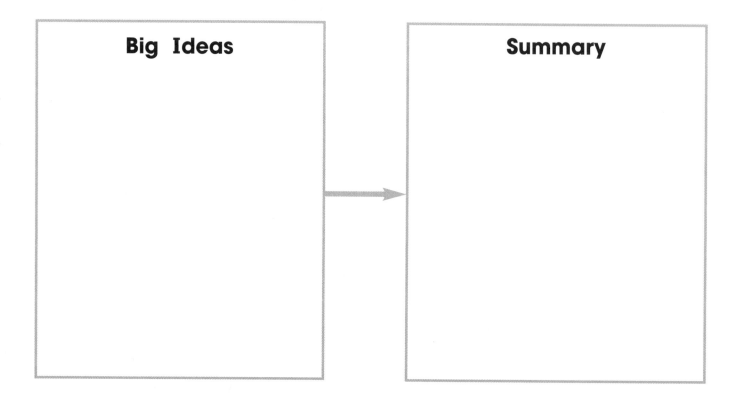

Big Ideas	**Summary**

Overview Summarizing Nonfiction

Directions and Sample Answers for Activity Pages

Day 1	See "Provide a Real-World Example" below.
Day 2	Ask students to tell a partner about the pictures. Then ask them to select and circle the best summary. (When you cut a circle, square, or diamond in half, you get a new shape.)
Day 3	Read and discuss the passage. Ask students to underline the big ideas. Then ask them to complete the sentence to write a summary. (**Big Ideas:** live in many places in the world, eat plants, fast, hard hooves. **Summary:** Deer are fast animals with hard hooves that live wherever they can find plants to eat.)
Day 4	Read and discuss the passage. Ask students to underline the big ideas. Then ask them to write a summary of the passage. (**Big Ideas:** telling time helps you plan, clock that shows 12:45, lunch is at 1:00, clock shows you how long you have to wait, almost time to get ready. **Summary:** Clocks help you know when to get ready for things that happen at a certain time.)
Day 5	Read the passage together. Ask students to write the big ideas and summary on their graphic organizers. Afterward, meet individually with students to discuss their results. Use their responses to plan further instruction and review. (**Big Ideas:** rocks under Earth's surface break apart and shift, ground shakes and moves, can cause serious damage, sometimes people are injured or killed, scientists cannot prevent earthquakes, can often predict when they will happen. **Summary:** Earthquakes shake and move the ground, which can cause serious damage, injuries, and death.)

Provide a Real-World Example

◆ Hand out the Day 1 activity page.

◆ **Say:** *I went shopping the other day to buy things for a dinner party. It would take a long time to tell you everything I bought. Instead, I'll tell you a summary:* **I bought a tablecloth, colorful napkins, and food for a dinner party.** *This summary tells the most important things I did in one sentence.*

◆ Pair students and ask them to summarize what they did the previous evening. Then **say:** *Look at the pictures on the page. Summarize the woman's shopping trip.* If students have difficulty, offer some suggestions, such as *A woman bought a vase and flowers to put in it.*

◆ Explain that students can also summarize information they read. Write the following on the chart paper:

Summarizing Nonfiction

Think about what you read.

Pick out the big ideas.

Write one or two sentences about the big ideas.

Something Special

Look at the pictures. Then summarize the events shown.

Cutting Shapes

Tell a partner about the pictures.

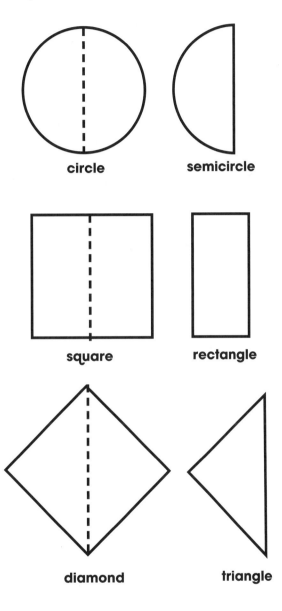

circle   semicircle

square   rectangle

diamond   triangle

Draw a circle around the best summary.

When you cut a shape in half, you get the same shape.

When you cut a circle, square, or diamond in half, you get a new shape.

When you cut a semicircle, rectangle, or triangle in half, you get a new shape.

Deer

Read the passage. Draw a line under the big ideas.

Deer live in many places in the world. They live
in lands that are cold and lands that are hot. They live
in deserts, mountains, and grassy plains.

Deer eat plants. They nibble on leaves, twigs, bark, and grass.
Sometimes they eat buds, berries, and other fruit.

Deer are fast, so they usually protect themselves by running away.
When they must fight, they kick their enemies with their hard hooves.
Male deer also fight with their antlers.

Complete the sentence to write a summary.

Deer are _____ animals with _____

that live wherever they can find _____ to eat.

It's Almost Time

Read the passage. Draw a line under the big ideas.

How old were you when you learned to tell time?
Telling time helps you plan.

Think of a clock that shows 12:45.
You know that lunch is at 1:00.

The clock shows you how long you have to wait.
It's almost time to get ready, because lunch is in
15 minutes!

Write a summary of the passage.

_____

_____

_____

_____

Assessment

Read the passage. Write the big ideas. Then write a summary.

Some places have earthquakes.

The rocks under Earth's surface break apart and shift.

The ground shakes and moves—sometimes a little, and sometimes a lot.

Mild earthquakes can be scary, but harmless.

Strong earthquakes can cause serious damage to streets, roads, bridges, and buildings.

Sometimes people are injured or killed.

Scientists study and measure the strength of earthquakes.

These scientists cannot prevent earthquakes.

However, they can often predict when they will happen.

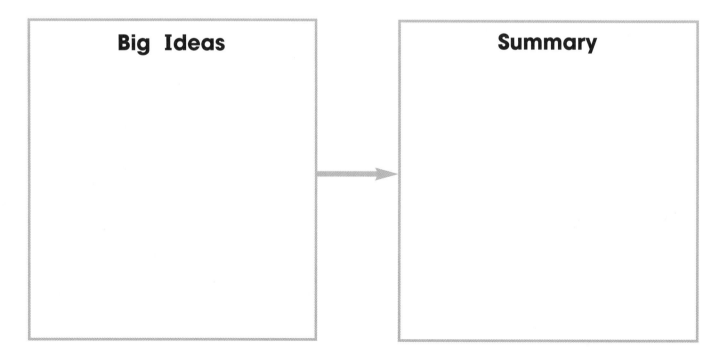

Big Ideas	**Summary**

Unit 12 • Everyday Comprehension Intervention Activities Grade 3 • ©2010 Newmark Learning, LLC

Overview Comparing and Contrasting in Fiction

Directions and Sample Answers for Activity Pages

Day 1	See "Provide a Real-World Example" below.
Day 2	Read and discuss the story. Then ask students to determine how Darla and Aiden are alike and different. (**Alike:** both like to watch TV, both know how to compromise, both like popcorn. **Different:** one prefers the TV channels, one prefers movies, one likes commercials.)
Day 3	Read and discuss the story. Then ask students to mark the chart by placing Xs in the appropriate columns to show how Todd and Jamal are alike and different. (**Todd:** likes to jump in and splash people, likes to play games in the water, likes to swim laps, has fun at the pool. **Jamal:** wants to be a better diver, has a sister, likes to play games in the water, has fun at the pool.)
Day 4	Read about Sue and Sam together. Discuss. Then ask students to circle the best answers. (**1:** both. **2:** Sue. **3:** Sam. **4:** Sue. **5:** both. **6:** Sam. **7:** Sue. **8:** Sam.)
Day 5	Read the story together. Ask students to write how Meg and Kenisha are alike and different on their graphic organizers. Afterward, meet individually with students to discuss their results. Use their responses to plan further instruction and review. (**Meg:** messy room, books and clothes on floor, can't find homework. **Kenisha:** neat room, books on shelf, clothes in closet. **Meg and Kenisha:** sisters, have their own rooms.)

Provide a Real-World Example

◆ Hand out the Day 1 activity page.

◆ **Say:** *I know some twins. They look exactly alike. They have the same color hair and eyes. They are the same size. But one likes to play games. She runs in her yard all day. The other likes to sit in the hammock and read. She is very quiet.*

◆ Ask students to look at the pictures of the twins. **Say:** *We can compare the twins. How are they alike?* Discuss. Then **say:** *We can contrast the twins. How are they different?* Discuss.

◆ Ask students to draw pictures of two people in their own families. Then invite them to share how these two people are alike and different.

◆ Explain that students can also compare and contrast things when they read stories. Write the following on chart paper:

Comparing and Contrasting in Fiction

Look at the pictures.

Think about the words.

See how things are alike. Look for words like *alike*, *too*, and *both*.

See how things are different. Look for words like *different*, *one*, and *but*.

Twins

Listen. Think about how the twins are alike and different.

Now draw or write about two people in your family. How are they alike and different?

Watching TV

Read the story.

"Let's watch TV," said Darla.

"OK!" said Aiden. "I'll get a DVD."

"But I want to watch the TV channels," said Darla. "Movies are too long."

"I hate watching TV channels," said Aiden. "Right when the show gets to a good part, a dumb commercial cuts in."

"I think the commercials are entertaining," said Darla.

"Let's compromise," said Aiden. "I'll watch TV shows with you today, and you can watch a movie with me tomorrow."

"Okay," said Darla. "I'll make popcorn today."

"I'll make some tomorrow, too," said Aiden.

How are Darla and Aiden the same? Draw a circle around the best answers.	**How are Darla and Aiden different? Draw a circle around the best answers.**
They both like to watch TV.	One likes to watch TV.
They both prefer the TV channels.	One prefers the TV channels.
They both prefer movies.	One prefers movies.
They both like commercials.	One likes commercials.
They both know how to compromise.	One knows how to compromise.
They both like popcorn.	One likes popcorn.

At the Pool

Read the story. Then mark the chart.

Todd and Jamal met at the pool. "Are you going to swim laps with me?" asked Todd.

"No, but I'm going to practice my diving," replied Jamal.

"Do you want to do some cannonball jumps and splash everyone in the deep end?" asked Todd.

"I'd better not," Jamal replied. "Last time I splashed my big sister, and she got really mad."

"I'm glad I don't have a big sister!" said Todd. "How about a game? I like the one where we toss in a penny and see who can find it first."

"I like that one, too," said Jamal. "Count me in!"

	Todd	**Jamal**
likes to jump in and splash people		
wants to be a better diver		
has a sister		
likes to play games in the water		
likes to swim laps		
has fun at the pool		

Sam and Sue

Read about Sam and Sue.

Sue walked through the parking lot after soccer practice. "Where are you going?" Sam asked.

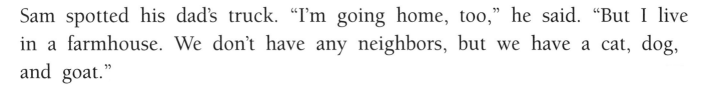

"Home," Sue replied. "I live in an apartment a couple of blocks away. It's right next to River School. I take the elevator to the fifth floor. Lots of people live in my building, and I know them all."

Sam spotted his dad's truck. "I'm going home, too," he said. "But I live in a farmhouse. We don't have any neighbors, but we have a cat, dog, and goat."

"That sounds like fun!" said Sue. "I'll see you at school tomorrow."

Draw a circle around the best answer.

1. Who plays soccer?	**Sam**	**Sue**	**both**
2. Who lives in a tall building?	**Sam**	**Sue**	**both**
3. Who has pets?	**Sam**	**Sue**	**both**
4. Who knows all the neighbors?	**Sam**	**Sue**	**both**
5. Who goes to River School?	**Sam**	**Sue**	**both**
6. Who needs a ride home?	**Sam**	**Sue**	**both**
7. Who can walk home?	**Sam**	**Sue**	**both**
8. Who probably rides a bus to school?	**Sam**	**Sue**	**both**

Assessment

Read the story. Then write how Meg and Kenisha are alike and different.

KNOCK! KNOCK! "Come in," called Meg.

Kenisha opened her sister's bedroom door and stopped in her tracks. "Your room is a mess!" she said. "Your books and clothes are all over the floor!"

"I can keep my room however I like it," said Meg.

"My room is neat," said Kenisha. "I know just where to find everything. My books are on the shelf, and my clothes are in the closet."

"You can keep your room however you like it, too," said Meg. "Now . . . can you help me find my homework?"

Meg	Meg and Kenisha	Kenisha

Overview Comparing and Contrasting in Nonfiction

Directions and Sample Answers for Activity Pages

Day 1	See "Provide a Real-World Example" below.
Day 2	Read and discuss the passage. Then ask students to determine how a vegetable and a flower are alike and different. (**Alike:** people like both of them, both are colorful, both grow in spring and summer, both can have weeds around their plants, both grow in gardens, both need water, both grow from seeds. **Different:** one is to eat, one has petals.)
Day 3	Read and discuss the passage. Then ask students to mark the chart by placing Xs in the appropriate columns to show how Acadia National Park and Big Bend National Park are alike and different. (**Acadia:** national park, has hikers, has visitors, near an ocean, has mountains, has bike paths, in Maine. **Big Bend:** near a river, national park, has hikers, has visitors, in Texas, has a desert, has mountains, has bike paths.)
Day 4	Read and discuss the passage. Then ask students to circle the best answers. (**1:** baseball. **2:** both. **3:** both. **4:** Go Fish. **5:** both. **6:** Go Fish. **7:** both. **8:** baseball.)
Day 5	Read the passage together. Ask students to write how city streets and dirt roads are alike and different on their graphic organizers. Afterward, meet individually with students to discuss their results. Use their responses to plan further instruction and review. (**City streets:** noisy, cars, trucks, buses, tall buildings, stoplights, lines to show people where to drive. **Dirt roads:** quiet, few vehicles, fences, fields, pastures. **City streets and dirt roads:** people can travel on them, people use them to get from place to place, people like to walk along them to enjoy the sights.)

Provide a Real-World Example

◆ Hand out the Day 1 activity page.

◆ **Say:** *I like to sit in a recliner when I read. My friend likes to sit in a large beanbag chair. My friend and I both sit in chairs, but the chairs are different. We can compare the two types of chairs by thinking about ways they are alike. We can contrast the two types of chairs by thinking of ways they are different.*

◆ Ask students to look at the pictures of the chairs. **Ask:** *How are the chairs alike? How are they different?* Repeat the activity with the pictures of the two tables.

◆ Invite students to draw two other pieces of furniture to compare and contrast. Then explain that they can also compare and contrast things when they read. Write the following on chart paper:

Comparing and Contrasting in Nonfiction

Look at the pictures.

Think about the words.

See how things are alike. Look for words like *alike, both, in common,* and *too.*

See how things are different. Look for words like *different, one, but, however, while, unlike,* and *on the other hand.*

Furniture

Look at each picture. How are they alike? How are they different?

**Draw two other pieces of furniture that are alike and different.
Tell a partner about them.**

Vegetables and Flowers

Read the passage.

You can grow vegetables in a garden.

Many people like to grow carrots, squash, and tomatoes.

Plant the seeds in spring. Water the seeds, and pull the weeds around the plants.

In summer, you'll have fresh, colorful vegetables to eat.

You can grow flowers in a garden, too.

Marigolds, daisies, and lilies are many people's favorites.

Plant the seeds in spring. Water the seeds, and pull the weeds around the plants.

In summer, you'll have beautiful, colorful petals to look at—but don't eat them!

How are a vegetable and a flower alike? Draw a circle around the best answers.

People like both of them.
Both are colorful.
Both grow in spring and summer.
Both are to eat.
Both can have weeds around
  their plants.
Both grow in gardens.
Both need water.
Both grow from seeds.
Both have petals.

How are a vegetable and a flower different? Draw a circle around the best answers.

People like one of them.
One is colorful.
One grows in spring and summer.
One is to eat.
One can have weeds around
  its plant.
One grows in a garden.
One needs water.
One grows from seeds.
One has petals.

Write one more way a vegetable and a flower are alike or different.

_____

National Parks

Read the passage. Then mark the chart.

Many people like to visit national parks. Each park is unique, or special. Acadia National Park is in Maine. You can climb on the rocks and watch the waves of the Atlantic Ocean crash in. Big Bend National Park is in Texas. You can go rafting in the Rio Grande. Both parks have paths for hiking and biking. Mountains are another feature they have in common. However, Big Bend has a desert, and Acadia doesn't.

	Big Bend Park	**Acadia Park**
near a river		
national park		
has hikers		
has visitors		
near an ocean		
in Texas		
has a desert		
has mountains		
has bike paths		
in Maine		

Outdoors and Indoors

Read the passage.

Outdoor games are fun. Indoor games are fun, too. Baseball is an outdoor game, but Go Fish is an indoor game. While you must have a large yard or ball field to play baseball, you can play Go Fish at the kitchen table. Both games have rules, and both games have a winner. You must gather many friends together to play baseball. On the other hand, you can play Go Fish with one friend. What are your favorite outdoor games? What games do you like to play indoors?

Draw a circle around the best answer.

1. You need to play in a large yard. **baseball**   **Go Fish**   **both**

2. People play this game.   **baseball**   **Go Fish**   **both**

3. This game is fun.   **baseball**   **Go Fish**   **both**

4. You can play at a table.   **baseball**   **Go Fish**   **both**

5. This game has a winner.   **baseball**   **Go Fish**   **both**

6. You can play with one friend.   **baseball**   **Go Fish**   **both**

7. This game has rules.   **baseball**   **Go Fish**   **both**

8. This game has many players.   **baseball**   **Go Fish**   **both**

Assessment

**Read the passage. Then write how city streets
and dirt roads are alike and different.**

People can travel on city streets and dirt
roads. Unlike dirt roads, city streets are
noisy. They are filled with cars, trucks, and
buses. You see tall buildings all around. You
see stoplights at the intersections, and the
streets have lines to show people where to
drive. On the other hand, dirt roads have
few vehicles. You often see fences, fields,
and pastures along these roads. City streets
and dirt roads have some things in
common. People use them to get from place
to place. People also like to walk along
them to enjoy the sights.

City Streets	City Streets and Dirt Roads	Dirt Roads

Overview Identifying Cause and Effect in Fiction

Directions and Sample Answers for Activity Pages

Day 1	See "Provide a Real-World Example" below.
Day 2	Read and discuss the sentences and pictures. Then ask students to draw or write an effect for each cause. (Jana will get an umbrella. Jana will use the umbrella. Jana will close the umbrella.)
Day 3	Read and discuss the sentences and pictures. Then ask students to draw or write a cause for each effect. (He sees a bag of dog treats. Someone threw a frisbee. He sees a squirrel. A big dog is walking by.)
Day 4	Read and discuss the story. Explain that some stories have more than one cause and effect. Then ask students to write each effect. (**First:** Mom told Clem not to touch anything. **Second:** He picked up a sparkly crystal vase. **Third:** He decided to hide the pieces. **Fourth:** He told the salesclerk what happened. **Fifth:** He didn't have to pay for the broken vase.)
Day 5	Read the story together. Ask students to write one of the causes and effects on their graphic organizers. Afterward, meet individually with students to discuss their results. Use their responses to plan further instruction and review. (**Cause:** Winter is coming. **Effect:** Leaves were falling and the air was cold. **Cause:** Soon there will be no food. **Effect:** The squirrels must look for acorns and seeds. **Cause:** The squirrels want to keep their acorns safe. **Effect:** They hide them in a tree. **Cause:** The squirrels want to keep their seeds safe. **Effect:** They hide them in a rock pile.)

Provide a Real-World Example

◆ Hand out the Day 1 activity page.

◆ **Say:** *One time, my car would not start. I had to call a repair person, and then I had to wait for the repair person to come. A cause is why something happens. What caused me to wait?* Allow time for students to respond. Then **say:** *An effect is what happens. What was the effect when the car would not start?*

◆ Write the words **cause** and **effect** on the board. Ask students to look at the pictures and write **cause** or **effect** under each picture as you discuss.

◆ Explain that students can also identify causes and effects when they read stories. Write the following on chart paper:

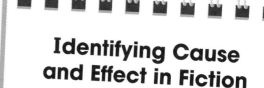

Identifying Cause and Effect in Fiction

Think about what made something happen.

Think about what happened and why.

Look for words like *because, so, if,* **and** *since.*

On the Road

Label each picture *cause* or *effect*.

_____

_____

_____

_____

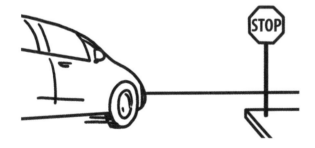

_____

_____

_____

_____

Rainy Day

Read the sentences. Look at the pictures.
Then draw or write an effect for each cause.

Jana saw rain clouds, so . . .

Jana had to go to the store in the rain, so . . .

The rain suddenly stopped, so . . .

Duke the Dog

Read the sentences. Look at the pictures.
Then draw or write a cause for each effect.

Duke the dog is happy, because . . .

Duke is running, because . . .

Duke is barking up a tree, because . . .

Duke is hiding, because . . .

The Gift Shop

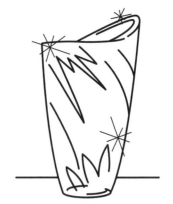

Read the story.

"Don't touch anything in the gift shop, because it might break," Mom warned.

"OK," said Clem.

Soon, Clem forgot Mom's rule and picked up a sparkly crystal vase. Crash! It fell onto the floor. "If I hide the pieces, no one will know I broke it," Clem thought.

"What are you doing?" asked a salesclerk.

Clem thought for a moment. He couldn't lie. "I broke a crystal vase," he said. "I'm sorry. I will pay for it."

"Since you were honest, you won't have to pay this time," said the salesclerk. "But why don't you sit on this bench and wait for your mom?"

Sometimes a story has many causes and effects. Write each effect.

Cause: The things in the gift shop might break.

Effect: _____

Cause: Clem forgot Mom's rule.

Effect: _____

Cause: Clem didn't want anyone to know he broke the vase.

Effect: _____

Cause: Clem couldn't lie.

Effect: _____

Cause: Clem was honest.

Effect: _____

Assessment

Read the story.
Then write one of the causes and effects.

Leaves were falling. The air was cold. Winter was coming! The squirrels had a meeting.

"Soon, there will be no food," said one squirrel. "So we must look for acorns and seeds."

"Here's an acorn. I will get it," said another squirrel. "And here's more. Where should we put them?"

"Hide them in the tree," said the first squirrel. "They will be safe there."

"We found some seeds," said some more squirrels. "We'll put them in the rock pile, since that's a safe place, too."

The first squirrel nodded approvingly. "If we hide plenty of acorns and seeds, we'll have enough to eat all winter," she said.

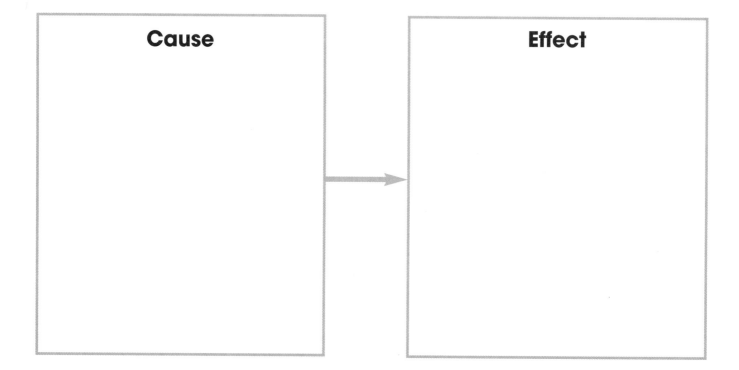

Cause	**Effect**

Overview Identifying Cause and Effect in Nonfiction

Directions and Sample Answers for Activity Pages

Day 1	See "Provide a Real-World Example" below.
Day 2	Read and discuss the sentences and pictures. Then ask students to draw or write an effect for each cause. (use a map; use a cell phone; look at a clock or watch)
Day 3	Read and discuss the sentences and pictures. Then ask students to draw or write a cause for each effect. (**Library:** they finished their book. **Restaurant:** they are hungry. **Laundry:** they have clothes to wash. **Store:** they need clothes to wear.)
Day 4	Read and discuss the passage. Explain that some passages have more than one cause and effect. Then ask students to write each effect. (**First:** They hang upside down. **Second:** They live in groups. **Third:** They hunt at night and sleep in the daytime. **Fourth:** They are different from all other mammals. **Fifth:** They fold an extra flap of skin between their feet into a pocket.)
Day 5	Read the passage together. Ask students to write one of the causes and effects on their graphic organizers. Afterward, meet individually with students to discuss their results. Use their responses to plan further instruction and review. (**Cause:** Spiders need a place to live. **Effect:** Spiders build webs. **Cause:** Spider webs are sticky. **Effect:** Insects get caught in the threads. **Cause:** The insects can't escape. **Effect:** The spider can eat them. **Cause:** An enemy touches the web. **Effect:** The spider feels the web shake. **Cause:** The spider feels the web shake. **Effect:** The spider can run away to a safer place.)

Provide a Real-World Example

◆ Hand out the Day 1 activity page.

◆ **Say:** *My friend loves violin music. A few years ago, she saw a poster about a violin concert. She immediately wrote the date of the concert on her calendar. A cause is why something happens. What caused my friend to write the date on her calendar?* Allow time for students to respond. Then **say:** *An effect is what happens. What was the effect of seeing the poster about the violin concert?*

◆ Write the words **cause** and **effect** on the board. Ask students to look at the pictures and write **cause** or **effect** under each picture as you discuss.

◆ Explain that students can also identify causes and effects when they read. Write the following on chart paper:

Identifying Cause and Effect in Nonfiction

Think about what made something happen.

Think about what happened and why.

Look for words like *because, so, if, since, why, in order to,* and *as a result.*

The Violin

Label each picture *cause* or *effect*.

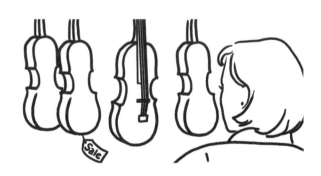

What Do They Do?

Read the sentences. Look at the pictures. Then draw or write an effect for each cause.

Sometimes people don't know how to get where they're going, so they . . .

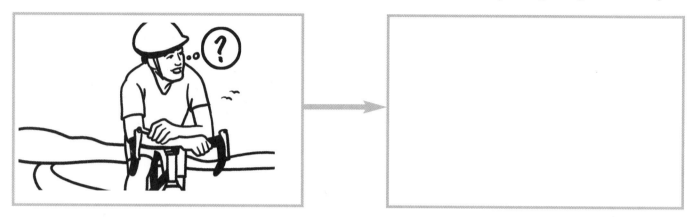

Sometimes people need to tell someone where to meet them, so they . . .

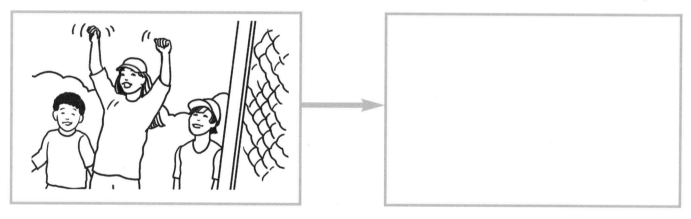

Sometimes people are not sure of the time, so they . . .

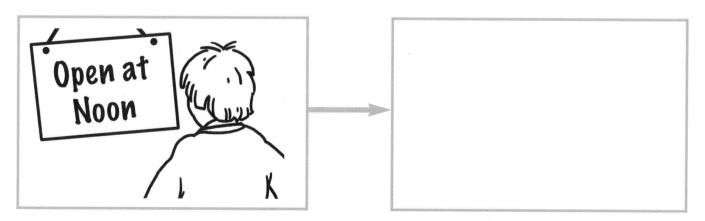

Why Do They Go?

Read the sentences. Look at the pictures. Then draw or write a cause for each effect.

People go to the library because . . .

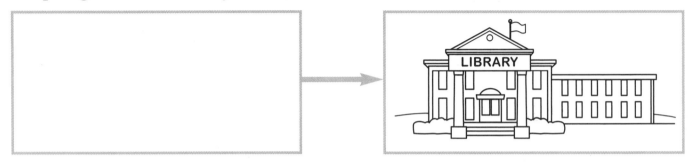

People go to a restaurant because . . .

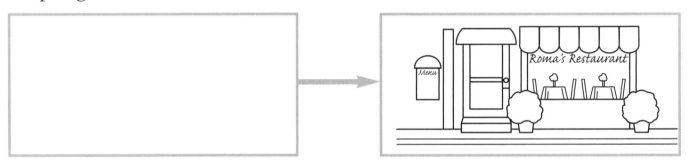

People go to the laundromat because . . .

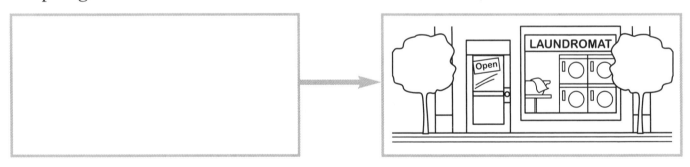

People go to a clothing store because . . .

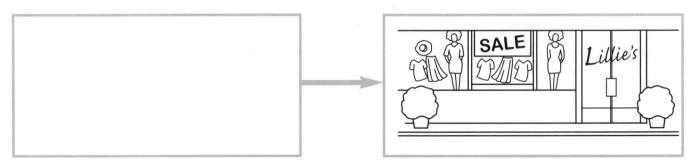

Bats

Read the passage.

Did you ever wonder why bats hang upside down? They're more comfortable that way! They can perch upright, but it takes a lot more effort. Since bats are social animals, they live in groups. Because they are nocturnal animals, they hunt at night and sleep in the daytime. Bats are mammals. However, they are different from all other mammals because they can fly. In order to catch insects while flying, many bats fold an extra flap of skin between their feet into a pocket. Now that's what I call fast food!

Sometimes a passage has many causes and effect. Write each effect.

Cause: Bats want to be comfortable.

Effect:_____

Cause: Bats are social animals.

Effect:_____

Cause: Bats are nocturnal animals.

Effect:_____

Cause: Bats can fly.

Effect:_____

Cause: Bats want to catch insects when they fly.

Effect:_____

Assessment

Read the passage.
Then write one of the causes and effects.

Spiders build webs. They live on their webs. A spider uses its web to get food. Because the web is sticky, insects get caught in the threads. Since the insects can't escape, the spider can eat them. A spider uses its web to stay safe, too. If an enemy touches the web, the spider feels the web shake. As a result, the spider can run away to a safer place.

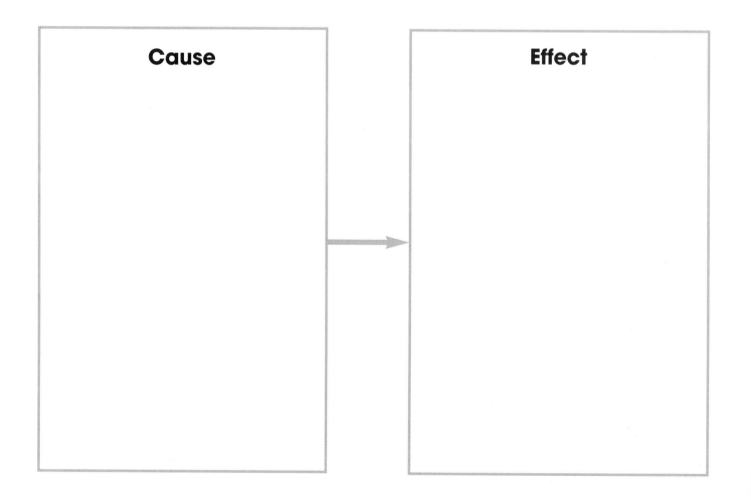

Cause	**Effect**

Overview   Making Inferences in Fiction

Directions and Sample Answers for Activity Pages

Day 1	See "Provide a Real-World Example" below.
Day 2	Discuss the pictures. Then ask students to circle the best inference for each picture. (The boy is planning a party. The girl is going to school. It is almost time for the movie to start. The boy is going to take photos.)
Day 3	Read and discuss the story. Then ask students to write their ideas in the boxes. (**Clues:** Willie feels better now. He needs to go to bed on time tonight. **Already Know:** People who go to bed late sometimes need a nap the next day. **Inference:** Willie just woke up from a nap. **Clues:** Willie and Dad are lying in the grass. They see a car and fish. **Already Know:** I can sometimes see shapes in the clouds. **Inference:** Willie and Dad are looking at the clouds.)
Day 4	Read and discuss the story. Then ask students to circle the best answer to each question. (**Clues:** The girls are dressed up. The girls are going to see their classmate, Jerrod. **Already Know:** People often dress up for special events. Sometimes people like to surprise their friends. **Inferences:** The girls are going to a surprise party for Jerrod. The girls are going to watch Jerrod perform in a play.)
Day 5	Read the story together. Ask students to write clues and what they already know about the clues. Then ask them to make an inference about what is happening. Afterward, meet individually with students to discuss their results. Use their responses to plan further instruction and review. (**Clues:** Rita stopped to chat with friends on the way home from school. Mom is looking at her watch. **Already Know:** Parents worry if their children get home late from school. **Inference:** Mom is worried because Rita took longer than usual to get home.)

Provide a Real-World Example

◆ Hand out the Day 1 activity page.

◆ **Say:** *I looked at my neighbor's car one day. A kayak was strapped to the roof of the car. The kayak is a clue. You already know something about boats like kayaks. Think about the clue and what you already know. Can you make a good guess, or inference, about where my neighbor was going?*

◆ Allow time for students to discuss their ideas and then complete the sentence. They should infer that your neighbor was going kayaking. However, point out that an inference isn't always correct. For example, your neighbor could have been moving the kayak for a friend or giving it away.

◆ Repeat the process with the other items on the page. Then explain that students can also make inferences when they read stories. Write the following on chart paper:

Making Inferences in Fiction

Find clues in the pictures.

Find clues in the words.

Think about what you already know.

Try to figure out what the author does not state.

My Neighbor Will...

Listen. Then make inferences for each picture.

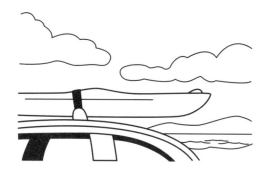

My neighbor will _____

_____ .

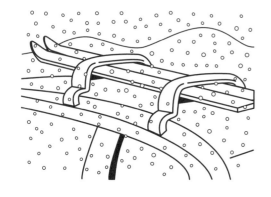

My neighbor will _____

_____ .

My neighbor will _____

_____ .

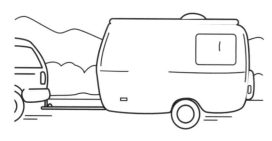

My neighbor will _____

_____ .

Look and Think

Draw a circle around the best inference for each picture.

The boy is planning a party.

The boy is planning a trip.

The girl is going to school.

The girl is going on a field trip.

The movie is over.

It is almost time for the movie to start.

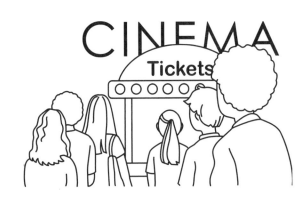

The boy is going to take photos.

The boy is looking for a good place to have a picnic.

Willie

Read about Willie.
Then write your ideas in the boxes.

"I feel much better now," said Willie.

"Great!" said Dad. "Now we can go for a hike. But tonight, you need to go to bed on time!"

> **I know from the text that . . .**
>
>

> **I already know . . .**
>
>

> **I can make an inference. Willie . . .**
>
>

Willie and Dad lay on the grass. "I see a car," Willie said.

"I don't see that," said Dad. "But I see a big fish."

> **I know from the text that . . .**
>
>

> **I already know . . .**
>
>

> **I can make an inference. Willie . . .**
>
>

All Dressed Up

Read the story.

Sandy twirled in front of the mirror. "You look great," said Keisha. "I really like that outfit."

"Thanks," said Sandy. "I couldn't decide what to wear. But when I saw what you were wearing, I decided to dress up, too."

"What time does it start?" asked Keisha.

"Two o'clock—we'd better ask my dad to take us in a few minutes," said Sandy.

"I can't wait!" said Keisha. "Jerrod will be so surprised to see our whole class there!"

Which clues are in the story? Draw a circle around the best answers.

The girls are dressed up.

The girls are going to be late.

The girls are going to see their classmate, Jerrod.

What do you already know? Draw a circle around the best answers.

Kids don't like to dress up.

People often dress up for special events.

Sometimes people like to surprise their friends.

Think about where the girls could be going.
Draw a circle around each possible inference.

The girls are going to a surprise party for Jerrod.

The girls are going to Jerrod's baseball game.

The girls are going to watch Jerrod perform in a play.

Assessment

Read about Rita. Write the clues and what you already know. Then write an inference.

"Wasn't today a great day at school?" asked Rita.

"Yes!" exclaimed Shamela. "Let's see . . . first we had that cool assembly . . . then we had the math test that everyone aced . . . then . . . "

Rita and Shamela walked and talked and talked and walked. Every few minutes, they stopped to chat with their other friends. Finally, they reached their corner and said good-bye as Shamela went left and Rita went right.

As Rita walked up the sidewalk, she saw her mom standing in the doorway looking at her watch. "Uh-oh . . . " thought Rita.

Clues	**What I Already Know**

Inference

Overview Making Inferences in Nonfiction

Directions and Sample Answers for Activity Pages

Day 1	See "Provide a Real-World Example" below.
Day 2	Discuss the pictures. Then ask students to make an inference about what they might do on each page and draw a circle around the best title. (**1:** Adding Triangles. **2:** Subtracting Squares. **3:** Multiplying Circles. **4:** Finishing a Pattern)
Day 3	Read and discuss the chart. Then ask students to write their ideas in the boxes and draw a picture to go with their inference. (**Evidence:** Kids are supposed to find out how long each activity takes. **Already Know:** We use a stopwatch to time activities. **Inference:** Kids will use a stopwatch to time each activity.)
Day 4	Read and discuss the journal entry. Then ask students to circle the best answer to each question. (**Evidence:** Two men brought something from the house to the truck. **Already Know:** Sometimes movers haul huge objects in trucks. **Inference:** The neighbors are moving away.)
Day 5	Read the passage together. Ask students to write evidence from the passage and what they already know about the evidence. Then ask them to make an inference about shells and beads long ago. Afterward, meet individually with students to discuss their results. Use their responses to plan further instruction and review. (**Evidence:** People used shells and beads to get wood, food, and clothing long ago. **Already Know:** The people needed wood, food, and clothing to survive. **Inference:** It was good to have a lot of shells and beads long ago.)

Provide a Real-World Example

◆ Hand out the Day 1 activity page.

◆ **Say:** *Yesterday I saw a friend getting into her car. She was dressed nicely and carrying a briefcase. The clothing and briefcase are evidence. You already know something about dressing nicely and carrying a briefcase, too. Think about the evidence and what you already know. Can you make a good guess, or inference, about where my friend was going?*

◆ Allow time for students to discuss their ideas and then complete the sentence. They should infer that your friend was going to work. However, point out that an inference isn't always correct. For example, she may have been going to a job interview or meeting.

◆ Repeat the process with the other pictures on the page. Then explain that students can also make inferences when they read. Write the following on chart paper:

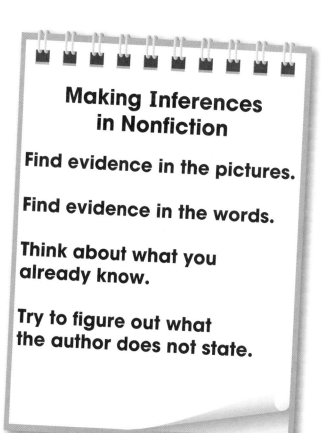

Making Inferences in Nonfiction

Find evidence in the pictures.

Find evidence in the words.

Think about what you already know.

Try to figure out what the author does not state.

Where Are They Going?

Listen. Then make inferences for each picture.

The woman is going

_____.

The man is going

_____.

The kids are going

_____.

The kids are going

_____.

Shape Math

Look at the pictures from a math book. Make an inference about what you might do on each page. Then draw a circle around the best title.

1.

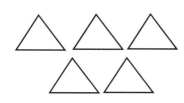 

    Adding Triangles   Subtracting Triangles

2.

    Adding Squares   Subtracting Squares

3.

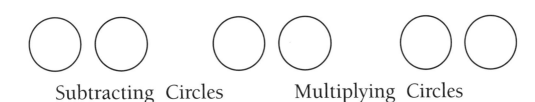

    Subtracting Circles   Multiplying Circles

4.

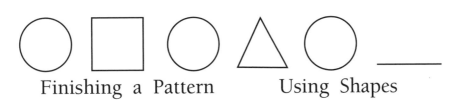

    Finishing a Pattern   Using Shapes

How Long?

Read the chart. Then write your ideas in the boxes.
Draw a picture to go with your inference.

How long does it take?	
activity	time
brushing teeth	
tying shoes	
eating breakfast	
cleaning room	

I know from the chart that . . .

I already know . . .

I can make an inference . . .

My Journal

Some people write in journals every day. Read the journal entry.

Tuesday, July 14

Something is going on next door. A big truck stopped in front of the house and two men got out.

First, they opened the back of the truck. Then they went inside the house. A while later, they came back out carrying something huge. It was all wrapped up. They put it in the truck, and then they went back into the house. I'm watching to see what happens next!

What evidence is in the journal entry? Draw a circle around the best answer.

Two men drove around the block looking for the house.

Two men brought something from the house to the truck.

Two men brought something from the truck to the house.

What do you already know? Draw a circle around the best answer.

Sometimes movers haul huge objects in trucks.

Movers only carry things that are wrapped.

People always use trucks to move things.

Which is the best inference? Draw a circle around the best answer.

The men are delivering new furniture to the house.

New neighbors are moving in.

The neighbors are moving away.

Assessment

Read the passage. Write the evidence from the passage. Write what you already know. Then write an inference.

Shells and beads are pretty to look at, but they were once very important, too. Long ago, people used shells and beads to buy things. They traded them for wood to make fires with, so they could cook food and keep warm. They also traded shells and beads to get food and clothing. People still trade things today. However, people buy most of the things they need with modern money, including coins and bills.

Evidence	**What I Already Know**

Inference

Overview Drawing Conclusions in Fiction

Directions and Sample Answers for Activity Pages

Day 1	See "Provide a Real-World Example" below.
Day 2	Read and discuss each character. Ask students to use the clues to draw a conclusion. Then ask them to draw a line to the right character. (**1:** boy at dentist. **2:** girl skiing. **3:** kids in line at a movie theater.)
Day 3	Read and discuss the story. Ask students to circle the best conclusion. Then ask them to circle the clues they used from the story. (**Conclusion:** Mrs. DeBetta is getting ready for the first day of school. **Clues:** classroom, new books, plant, desks, a good year, supplies.)
Day 4	Read and discuss the story. Ask students to write a conclusion about Ellen. Then ask them to draw a line under the clues they used from the story. (**Conclusion:** Ellen decided that it was not right to go to the pond. **Clues:** Ellen looked at Sonia. Sonia looked sad. Ellen grinned and patted Sonia's arm. "It's okay. We can play at my house.")
Day 5	Read the story together. Ask students to write clues from the story on their graphic organizers. Then ask them to write a conclusion. Afterward, meet individually with students to discuss their results. Use their responses to plan further instruction and review. (**Clues:** don't know how to make grilled cheese sandwiches, don't know how to use the stove, don't know how to turn on the microwave, having a bowl of cereal and an apple. **Conclusion:** The girls don't know how to cook.)

Provide a Real-World Example

◆ Hand out the Day 1 activity page.

◆ **Say:** *What happens when you try to decide what present to buy a friend? You think about what your friend likes to do. Does the friend have a hobby? Does the friend like to read? Does the friend collect something? All of these things are clues. You can use the clues to figure out a good present for your friend.*

◆ Tell students that using several clues to figure something out is called drawing a conclusion. Ask them to draw a picture of a present for someone. Then help them fill in the clues about the present. One at a time, ask students to read their clues to the class. Once the class draws the correct conclusion about the present, invite the student to share the picture.

◆ Explain that students can also draw conclusions when they read stories. Write the following on chart paper:

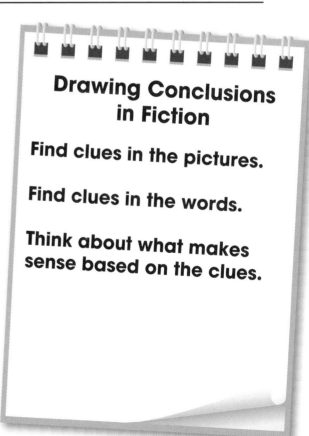

Drawing Conclusions in Fiction

Find clues in the pictures.

Find clues in the words.

Think about what makes sense based on the clues.

A Present

Draw a present below. Then write clues about the present.

Clues:

1. This present is for someone who spends time on

_____.

2. The person likes to

_____.

3. The person talks about

_____.

Name _____

What's Going On?

Read about each character. Use the clues to draw a conclusion. Then draw a line to the right character.

1. "I'm not sure about this," said Dennis.

   "Mom said it wouldn't hurt. I hope she was right!

   Next time, I'm erasing the appointment from the calendar.

   But at least the chair is comfortable."

2. "I did it!" cried Sue. "I knew I could.

   I just had to be patient and learn the right way.

   I only fell down twice, too.

   Now I'm ready for some hot chocolate!"

3. "I hope we can get in," said Jenna.

   "We've been waiting so long.

   I hope this is as good as the book!

   Especially since I'm spending my whole allowance on the ticket."

Getting Ready

Read the story.

"Here we go!" Mrs. DeBetta said to her helper, Carl. She opened the door of the classroom and looked around. Then she pointed to the windowsill. "There's a nice sunny spot for my plant."

"Should I put the desks in rows or groups?" asked Carl.

"Let's put them in groups," Mrs. DeBetta replied.

"After that, I'll get the new books out of this box for you," said Carl.

"Great!" said Mrs. DeBetta. "And I see that we have plenty of supplies."

"This will be a good year!" said Carl.

Which is the best conclusion? Draw a circle around your answer.

Mrs. DeBetta is a science teacher.

Carl is one of Mrs. DeBetta's students.

Mrs. DeBetta is getting ready for the first day of school.

Mrs. DeBetta is cleaning out her classroom at the end of the year.

Which clues for the conclusion are in the story? Draw a circle around your answers.

classroom	plans	pencils	desks
new books	teachers	students	a good year
markers	principal	plant	supplies

Ellen

Read the story.

"Let's go to the pond to swim!" said Ellen.

"We can fish there, too."

"I have to get permission first," said Sonia.

"But my mom is at work right now."

"That's not fair!" said Ellen.

"MY mom said we could go. And my big sister would come with us."

Ellen looked at Sonia. Sonia looked sad.

Ellen grinned and patted Sonia's arm.

"It's okay," she said. "We can play at my house.

We'll go to the pond tomorrow if your mom says it's okay."

What can you conclude about Ellen?

_____

_____

_____

Draw a line under the clues you used to draw a conclusion.

Assessment

**Read the story. Write the clues from the story.
Then write a conclusion.**

Keisha and her sister Amanda went to the
kitchen. "I'm hungry! Let's have some grilled
cheese sandwiches," said Keisha.

"We don't know how to make that," said Amanda.

"We could heat some soup," Keisha suggested.

"We don't know how to use the stove," Amanda replied.

"Can we warm up some leftovers from last night's dinner?" asked Keisha.

"We don't know how to turn on the microwave," Amanda answered.

"Hmm . . ." said Keisha. "How about a bowl of cereal and an apple?"

"Yum!" said Amanda.

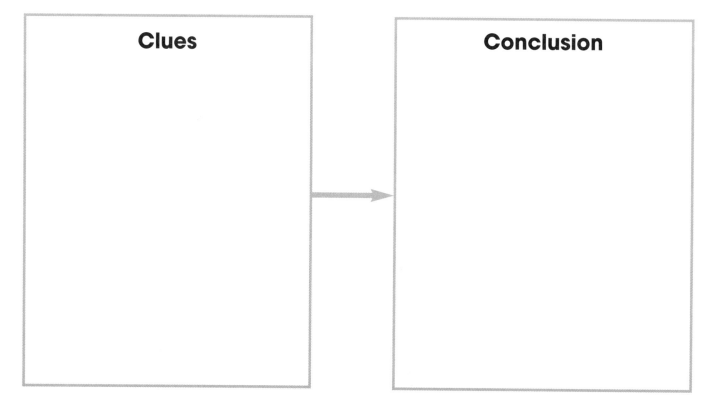

Clues	Conclusion

Overview Drawing Conclusions in Nonfiction

Directions and Sample Answers for Activity Pages

Day 1	See "Provide a Real-World Example" below.
Day 2	Read and discuss the sentences and pictures. Then ask students to draw a circle around the best conclusion for each set. (**First:** Some people paint pictures in art class. **Second:** People can make different things from clay.)
Day 3	Read and discuss the passage. Ask students to circle the best conclusion. Then ask them to circle the evidence they used from the passage. (**Conclusion:** People find minerals in many places on Earth. **Evidence:** in our food, on Earth, in mines, in rocks, in the sea, in the ground, in caves.)
Day 4	Read and discuss the passage. Ask students to write a conclusion about the ice resurfacer. Then ask them to draw a line under the evidence they used from the passage. (**Conclusion:** The ice resurfacer makes the ice better for skaters. **Evidence:** has a job to do, makes the ice smooth, no more bumps or cracks, skate faster now.)
Day 5	Read the passage together. Ask students to write evidence from the passage on their graphic organizers. Then ask them to write a conclusion. Afterward, meet individually with students to discuss their results. Use their responses to plan further instruction and review. (**Evidence:** stays with her baby for about a year, feeds her baby, baby follows her, keeps baby safe, teaches baby how to breathe. **Conclusion:** Mother whales take good care of their babies.)

Provide a Real-World Example

◆ Hand out the Day 1 activity page.

◆ **Say:** *Imagine you see a woman. She is standing at a corner near a school. She is wearing an orange vest. She tells some children when to cross the street. She stops the cars so the children can cross safely. All these things you see are evidence. You can use the evidence to figure out that the woman is a crossing guard.*

◆ Tell students that using several pieces of evidence to figure something out is called drawing a conclusion. Ask them to draw pictures of people doing their jobs. Then ask them to fill in the evidence about the people. One at a time, ask students to read their evidence to the class. Once the class draws the correct conclusions about the jobs, invite the student to share the pictures.

◆ Explain that students can also draw conclusions when they read. Write the following on chart paper:

Drawing Conclusions in Nonfiction

Find evidence in the pictures.

Find evidence in the words.

Think about what makes sense based on the evidence.

Hard at Work

Draw pictures of people doing their jobs. Then write evidence about their jobs.

Evidence:

1. This person _____

_____.

2. This person _____

_____.

3. This person _____

_____.

Evidence:

1. This person _____

_____.

2. This person _____

_____.

3. This person _____

_____.

Art Class

Read the sentences. Look at each group of pictures. Think about the evidence in the words and pictures. Then draw a circle around the best conclusion.

People like to make things in art class.

Conclusion:

People only paint pictures in art class.

Some people paint pictures in art class.

People always frame the pictures they paint.

Some people make things from clay.

 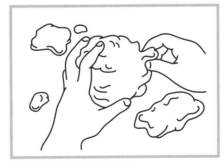 

Conclusion:

Making things from clay is hard work.

Painters do not make things from clay.

People can make different things from clay.

Minerals

Read the passage.

Minerals are on Earth, but they are not living creatures. Some minerals are metals, and some minerals are gems. People use gems to make beautiful jewelry. Minerals can be hard or soft. They can be shiny or dull. They can be clear or colorful. We find minerals in rocks, in the ground, and in caves. We find minerals in the sea and in mines. We even find minerals in our food!

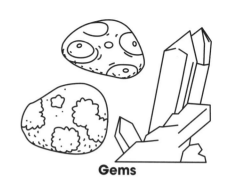

Gems

Which is the best conclusion? Draw a circle around your answer.

All minerals look and feel the same.

The most important minerals are gems.

People find minerals in many places on Earth.

Minerals are the only nonliving objects on Earth.

What evidence for the conclusion is in the passage?
Draw a circle around your answers.

jewelry	in rocks
in our food	in the sea
soft	gems
on Earth	metals
in mines	in the ground
shiny	clear
living creatures	in caves

On the Ice

Read the passage.

A whistle blows. "Everyone off the ice!" calls the rink director.

A big machine called an ice resurfacer has a job to do.

Frank Zamboni invented the ice resurfacer in 1949.

As a result, many people call all ice resurfacers Zambonis.

The ice resurfacer rolls over the surface of the ice. It makes the ice smooth.

Soon, the ice has no more bumps or cracks.

The skaters can come back now. They can skate faster now, too!

What is one thing you can conclude about the ice resurfacer?

_____

_____

_____

Draw a line under the evidence you used to draw your conclusion.

Assessment

Read the passage. Write the evidence from the passage. Then write a conclusion.

A mother whale stays with her baby for about a year.

She feeds her baby milk from her body.

The baby follows her wherever she goes.

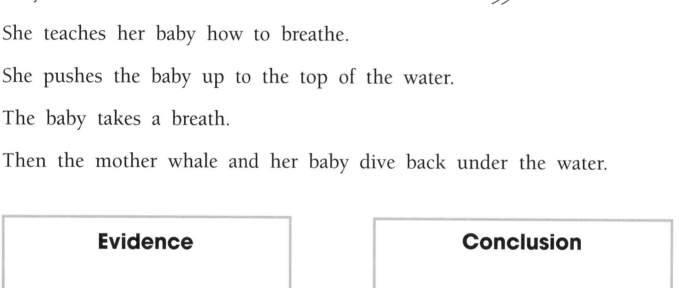

The mother does her best to keep her baby safe.

She teaches her baby how to breathe.

She pushes the baby up to the top of the water.

The baby takes a breath.

Then the mother whale and her baby dive back under the water.

Evidence	**Conclusion**

Overview Evaluating Author's Purpose in Fiction

Directions and Sample Answers for Activity Pages

Day 1	See "Provide a Real-World Example" below.
Day 2	Read and discuss the back-cover blurbs. Then ask students to circle the author's purpose for each one and draw a picture that might be in one of the books. (entertain readers by telling a story from long ago; entertain readers with a funny story about aliens)
Day 3	Read and discuss the riddles. Then ask students to complete the sentence about the author's purpose and draw a picture about one of the riddles. (The author probably wants to entertain readers with funny animal riddles.)
Day 4	Read and discuss the story. Then ask students to write the author's purpose and underline the clues in the story. (**Author's Purpose:** to entertain readers with a tall tale. **Clues:** slept outside under the stars, travel the country, feet are already as tough as an elephant's hide, plant apple trees everywhere I go, made a coat out of an old sack, put a tin pan on his head, the whole country is my orchard.)
Day 5	Read the poem together. Ask students to write clues about the author's purpose on the graphic organizer. Then ask them to record the author's purpose. Afterward, meet individually with students to discuss their results. Use their responses to plan further instruction and review. (**Clues:** The author uses lots of big words to brag and then says the reflection in the mirror has spinach on its tooth. **Author's Purpose:** to entertain readers with a silly poem.)

Provide a Real-World Example

◆ Hand out the Day 1 activity page.

◆ **Say:** *My friend and I watched a movie on DVD. It was funny! The characters kept trying to get themselves out of trouble. The things they said and did made us laugh. From these clues, I could tell that the actors wanted to entertain the audience.*

◆ Ask students to Think/Pair/Share a DVD they think is entertaining. Then **say:** *Write the name of the DVD on your paper. Then draw a scene from the show. Be sure the scene shows why the DVD is so entertaining.* Allow time for students to share their scenes with the class.

◆ Explain that they can also evaluate an author's purpose when they read stories. Write the following on chart paper:

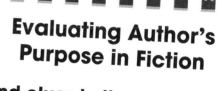

Evaluating Author's Purpose in Fiction

Find clues in the pictures.

Find clues in the words.

Think like the author.

Think about how the author tries to entertain.

Movie Time

Think of a movie that is entertaining. Then draw a fun scene from the movie.

Title of Movie: _____

Stories

Look at the blurb on the back of each book. Then draw a circle around the best answer to the question.

In this book, the author probably wants to:

entertain readers by telling a story from long ago

persuade readers to visit a castle

In this book, the author probably wants to:

inform readers how spaceships work

entertain readers with a funny story about aliens

Draw a picture that might be in one of the books.

Animal Guessing Game

Read the riddles. Then complete the sentence.

What do giraffes have that no other animal has?
Baby giraffes!

Should you write a report on a lion?
No—you should write a report on paper!

Why do elephants have trunks?
To use on vacation!

What kind of stories do dogs like best?
Tall tails!

The author probably wants to _____

_____.

Draw a picture about one of the riddles.

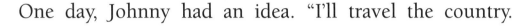

Johnny Appleseed

Read the story.

Johnny Appleseed loved his family's orchard.

He spent his days outdoors walking barefoot in the grass and tending the apple trees.

He even slept outside under the stars.

One day, Johnny had an idea. "I'll travel the country.

My feet are already as tough as an elephant's hide.

I'll head west, and I'll plant apple trees everywhere I go."

He made a coat out of an old sack.

He put a tin pan on his head to use for a hat and cooking pot.

He took a sack of apple seeds, and off he went.

"Now, the whole country is my orchard," he said.

The author's purpose is _____

_____.

Draw a line under the clues in the story.

Assessment

Read the poem. Write the clues. Then write the author's purpose.

I look into the mirror,
and I'm amazed to see
a most impressive person
gazing back at me.
This person's quite amazing,
extraordinary, too!
Brilliant, clever, striking,
notable—who knew?
Outstanding and inspiring—
but just a bit uncouth . . .
my mortified reflection
has spinach on its tooth!

Clues	Author's Purpose

Overview Evaluating Author's Purpose in Nonfiction

Directions and Sample Answers for Activity Pages

Day 1	See "Provide a Real-World Example" below.
Day 2	Read and discuss the blurbs. Then ask students to circle the author's purpose for each one and draw a picture that might be in one of the brochures. (inform readers where to recycle, persuade readers to recycle, inform people how to reuse household items)
Day 3	Read and discuss the directions and sign. Then ask students to circle the author's main purpose for each one. (The author is informing readers how to make clay. The author is persuading readers to come visit the craft shop.)
Day 4	Read and discuss the book review. Help students answer the first question and color the evidence blue. Then help them answer the second question and color the evidence red. (**1.** the book. **Evidence:** all but the first and last line. **2:** read the book. **Evidence:** first line, last line.)
Day 5	Read the passage. Ask students to write evidence about the author's purpose on the graphic organizer. Then ask them to record the author's purpose. Afterward, meet individually with students to discuss their results. Use their responses to plan further instruction and review. (**Evidence:** Every sentence describes or tells a fact about germs. **Author's Purpose:** to inform readers about germs.)

Provide a Real-World Example

◆ Hand out the Day 1 activity page.

◆ **Say:** *I recently watched a cooking show. Some chefs baked a cake step by step. They explained each step and told why it was important. They also gave the viewers baking tips. From this evidence, I could tell that the chefs wanted to inform viewers about the best way to bake a cake.*

◆ Ask students to Think/Pair/Share shows they have seen that give viewers information. Then **say:** *Write what you learned from one of these shows. Then draw a picture.* Allow time for students to share their pictures.

◆ Explain that they can also evaluate an author's purpose when they read. Write the following on chart paper:

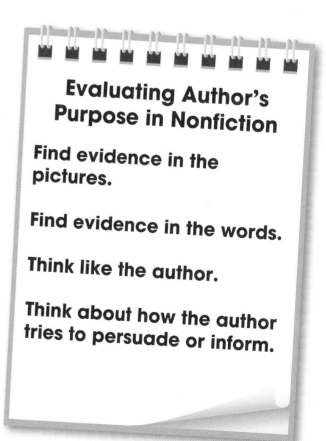

Evaluating Author's Purpose in Nonfiction

Find evidence in the pictures.

Find evidence in the words.

Think like the author.

Think about how the author tries to persuade or inform.

Informational TV

Think of a TV show that is educational. Write and draw about what you learned.

TV Show: _____

From this show, I learned

_____

_____ .

Recycle and Reuse

Look at the blurb on the front of each brochure. Then draw a circle around the best answer to the question.

In this brochure, the author probably wants to:

inform readers where to recycle

persuade readers to recycle

In this brochure, the author probably wants to:

inform people about the planets

persuade readers to recycle

In this brochure, the author probably wants to:

inform people how to reuse household items

persuade readers to recycle

Draw a picture that might be in one of the brochures.

Roll It Out

You can make your own clay. Read the directions.

1. Get one cup of salt.

2. Mix with 2 cups of flour.

3. Add ¾ cup of water.

4. Mix with your hands.

5. Roll out the dough.

6. Make something for a friend!

What is author's main purpose? Draw a circle around the best answer.

The author is informing readers how to make clay.

The author is persuading readers to make things with clay.

The author is entertaining readers with a story about making a mess with flour and water.

Read the sign.

> # Create your own pots!
>
> **Make gifts for your friends!**
>
> **It's easy! It's fun!**
>
> **Best crafts in town!**

What is the author's purpose? Draw a circle around the best answer.

The author is informing readers about gift ideas.

The author is persuading readers to come visit the craft shop.

The author is entertaining readers with a funny sign.

The Long Journey

Read the book review. Then answer the questions.

The Long Journey is an exciting book!

It is about a family traveling west long ago.

The family rides in a covered wagon.

The book tells what the family ate.

It tells how they slept and played.

It tells about the dangers on the trip.

The family faced terrible storms and even a buffalo stampede.

Give this book a try. You won't be able to put it down!

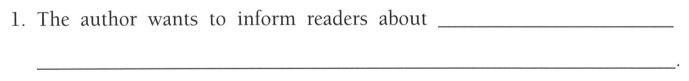

1. The author wants to inform readers about _____

   _____.

   Color this evidence blue.

2. The author wants to persuade readers to _____

   _____.

   Color this evidence red.

Assessment

Read the passage. Write the evidence. Then write the author's purpose.

Germs are living things.

They live in many places, both outdoors and indoors.

Germs are so small you can't see them.

Most germs won't hurt you, but some germs can make you sick.

To protect yourself and others from these germs, wash your hands often.

Cover your mouth when you cough or sneeze.

It's also wise to stay away from other people who are already sick.

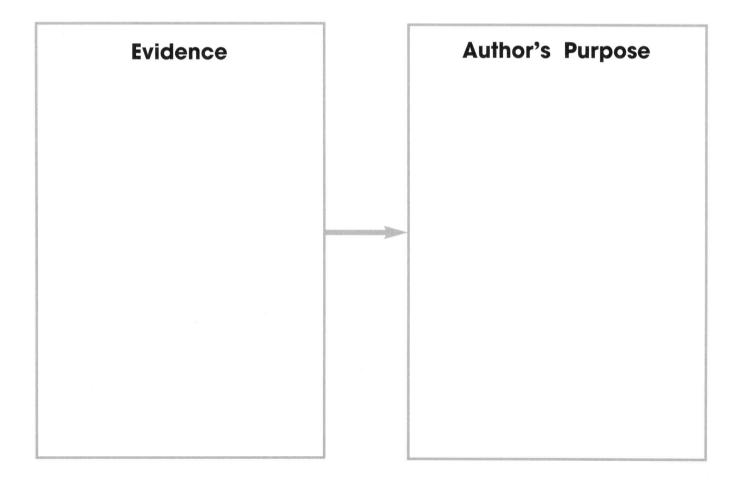

Evidence

Author's Purpose

Overview Analyzing Text Structure and Organization in Fiction

Directions and Sample Answers for Activity Pages

Day 1	See "Provide a Real-World Example" below.
Day 2	Read the sentences and discuss the pictures. Then ask students to draw a circle around the main text structure for each set. (Sequence of Events, Problem and Solution, Compare and Contrast)
Day 3	Read the sentences and discuss the pictures. Then ask students to draw a line to the name of the main text structure. (**1:** Compare and Contrast. **2:** Sequence of Events. **3:** Problem and Solution.)
Day 4	Read about Janelle. Then ask students to follow the directions in each box. (Responses will vary.)
Day 5	Read the story together. Ask students to write clues on the graphic organizer. Then ask them to name the main text structure. Afterward, meet individually with students to discuss their results. Use their responses to plan further instruction and review. (**Clues:** Caitlyn gets a present. She finds her aunt's phone number. She calls her aunt. She leaves a message. **Text Structure:** Sequence of Events.)

Provide a Real-World Example

◆ Hand out the Day 1 activity page.

◆ **Say:** *Last summer, I had a letter from a young friend. She was at sleepaway camp. She told me what she did every day. She told me about her new friends. She told me what it was like to sleep outdoors. She even told me how the food at the camp tasted. From these clues, I could tell my friend was describing her experiences at camp.*

◆ Ask students to read the description of sleeping outdoors on their page. Then ask them to draw a picture based on the description. Allow time for students to compare their drawings with their classmates.

◆ **Say:** *Description is one type of text structure we find when we read stories. We also find four other text structures.* Write the following on chart paper:

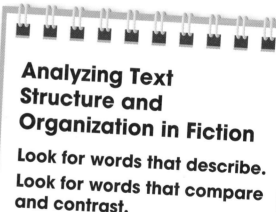

Analyzing Text Structure and Organization in Fiction

Look for words that describe.

Look for words that compare and contrast.

Look for words that tell about cause and effect.

Look for words that tell about a sequence of events.

Look for words that tell about a problem and a solution.

Sleeping Outdoors

Read the description. Then draw a picture based on what you have read.

I lie in my cozy sleeping bag and look up.

A large branch creates a roof over my head.
Between the leaves, I see twinkling stars.

The moon is a glowing orange on a dark blue plate.

A gentle breeze blows across my face.

I hear the soft noises of the forest at night.

I feel the warmth of the campfire.

I can't imagine a nicer moment.

Can you?

Bee Power

**Read the sentences. Look at each group of pictures. Think about the clues.
Then draw a circle around the main text structure.**

"Flowers! Here I come!" said Bee.

Text Structure:

Description

Sequence of Events

Compare and Contrast

Cause and Effect

Problem and Solution

"Hmm . . . who was here first?" thought Bee.

Text Structure:

Description

Sequence of Events

Compare and Contrast

Cause and Effect

Problem and Solution

"Sunflowers or daisies?" wondered Bee.

Text Structure:

Description

Sequence of Events

Compare and Contrast

Cause and Effect

Problem and Solution

The Party

**Read the sentences. Look at the pictures. Think about the clues.
Then draw a line to the name of the main text structure.**

1. "My gift is a game,"
said Sarah.

"My gift is a model,"
said Cai.

"Cal is going to love
his party!"

Description

**Sequence
of Events**

2. "Squeeze the lemon, Cal,"
said Mom.

"Now add the water. Put
in some sugar, and mix
it up.

Good job! Now we have
lemonade for your party."

**Compare
and Contrast**

**Cause
and Effect**

3. "Uh-oh . . . I dropped
my piece of cake!"
said Cai.

"I'll get a paper towel,"
said Sarah.

"I'll get a broom and
dustpan," said Cal.
"No harm done!"

**Problem
and Solution**

Janelle's Train Set

Read about Janelle's train set.

Janelle got out her train set.

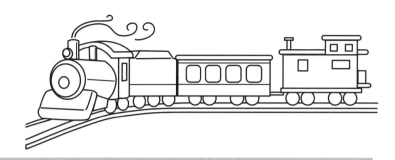

Description: Write three sentences that describe the train set.

Sequence of Events: Write how to put a train set together.

Compare and Contrast: Write about two types of cars on the train set.

Cause and Effect: Write what can happen when the train goes too fast.

Problem and Solution: Janelle can't find the train station that goes with her set. What should she do?

Assessment

Read the story. Write clues from the story. Then name the main text structure.

"Look, Mom!" exclaimed Caitlyn. "Aunt Amy sent me a present. Can I call her to say thanks?"

"Sure!" Mom replied. "But you'll need to find her number first."

"Here it is," said Caitlyn. "I'll dial it now." Caitlyn listened and waited. "Aunt Amy must not be home," she said.

"Listen for the beep, then you can leave a message," said Mom.

"I hear the beep!" whispered Caitlyn. "I'll start now."

Caitlyn spoke clearly into the phone. "Hello, Aunt Amy! It's me— Caitlyn. Thank you sooooooo much for the present. It's just what I wanted. You're the best aunt ever!"

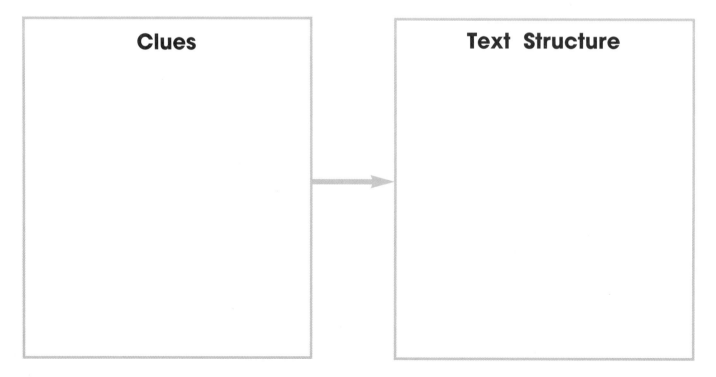

Clues	Text Structure

Overview Analyzing Text Structure and Organization in Nonfiction

Directions and Sample Answers for Activity Pages

Day 1	See "Provide a Real-World Example" below.
Day 2	Read the passage and discuss the pictures. Then ask students to draw a circle around the correct text structures. (Description, Compare and Contrast)
Day 3	Read and discuss the passages. Then help students write the names of the main text structures on the lines. (Problem and Solution, Cause and Effect)
Day 4	Read about community workers. Then ask students to follow the directions in each box. (Responses will vary.)
Day 5	Read the sign together. Ask students to write evidence on the graphic organizer. Then ask them to name the main text structure. Afterward, meet individually with students to discuss their results. Use their responses to plan further instruction and review. (**Evidence:** Each word and phrase tells something about the yard sale. **Text Structure:** Description.)

Provide a Real-World Example

◆ Hand out the Day 1 activity page.

◆ **Say:** *I recently read an article about building a tree house. First, you buy the wood. Then you measure and cut the wood. After that, you build a box-type structure in the branches of a tree. Finally, you build a ladder to use to get to the tree house. From this evidence, I knew the text structure was a sequence of events. In a how-to text, we also call this text structure steps in a process.*

◆ Ask students to number the pictures on the page to show the correct order. Then ask them to read the passage and draw pictures to show a sequence of events. Allow time for students to share their drawings.

◆ **Say:** *Sequence of events is one type of text structure we find when we read. We also find four other text structures.* Write the following on chart paper:

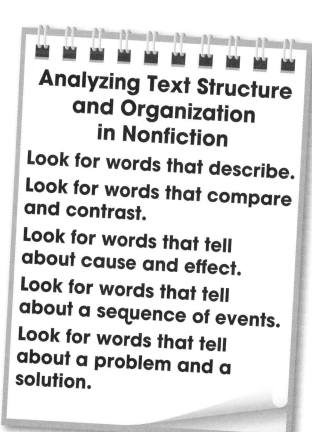

Analyzing Text Structure and Organization in Nonfiction

Look for words that describe.

Look for words that compare and contrast.

Look for words that tell about cause and effect.

Look for words that tell about a sequence of events.

Look for words that tell about a problem and a solution.

The Tree House

Listen. Then number the pictures in the correct order.

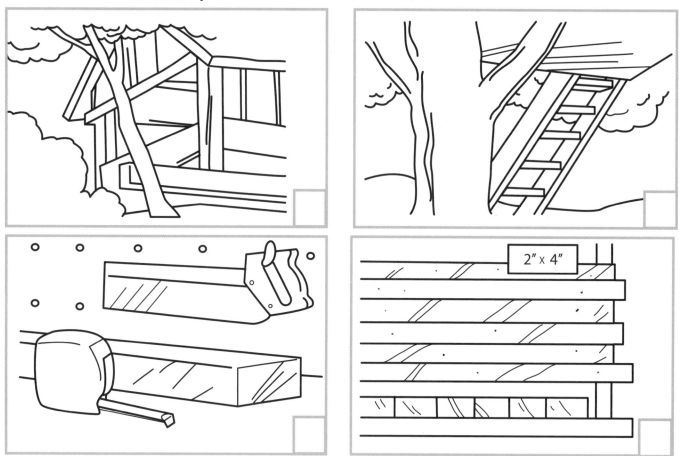

Read the passage. Then draw the sequence of events based on what you have read.

We had a sleepover in the new tree house. First, we got a flashlight, our sleeping bags, and some snacks. Then we climbed up to the treehouse. We told stories for a while. Finally, we fell asleep.

All Kinds of Weather

Read the passage. Look at the pictures.

Do you have different kinds of weather where you live?
Most people like sunny days best.
Some people like rainy days, too.
Lots of people like snowy days!

You can play outside on sunny days.
You can go bike riding and play ball at the park.
You can go to the beach or have a noisy game in the backyard.

On rainy days, you stay indoors.
You can read books and watch movies.
You can play games at the kitchen table or on the computer.

Some people stay indoors on snowy days.
Other people love to go outdoors and build snowmen.
Which would you do?

**This passage uses two text structures. Think about the evidence.
Then draw a circle around the correct text structures.**

Text Structure:

Description

Sequence of Events

Compare and Contrast

Cause and Effect

Problem and Solution

Everyday Math

**Read the passages. Think about the evidence.
Then write the name of the main text structure on the line.**

Word Bank

| Description | Sequence of Events | Compare and Contrast |

| Cause and Effect | Problem and Solution |

Your teacher assigns your group a book to read. You decide that each team member will read some of the pages. Then the team members will teach the rest of the group what they learn. But how many pages should each team member read? How can you make it fair? See how many pages are in the book. Divide that number by the number of team members.

_____

Long ago, people measured things with their feet and hands. As a result, their measurements were different. For example, one person's "two feet long" could be several inches shorter than another person's "two feet long." Now that we have rulers, metersticks, and other standard measuring tools, people can rely on each other's measurements.

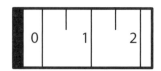

_____

Community Workers

Read about community workers.

A community needs many workers to help
it operate smoothly. Some people provide
transportation. Some people keep the
community safe. Some people care for
people who are sick. Others build homes, sell food and clothing,
or care for small children while their parents work. Every worker
is important!

Description: Think of a community worker you have seen in action.
Write three sentences that describe the person's job.

Sequence of Events: A teacher is a community worker. Write how
someone becomes a teacher.

Compare and Contrast: Think of two jobs you might like to have
someday. Tell how the jobs are alike and different.

Cause and Effect: Sometimes a new business comes to a community.
Write about how the business might change the community.

Problem and Solution: Sometimes a bad storm damages a community.
Write about how the community workers can help.

Assessment

Read the sign. Write evidence from the sign. Then name the main text structure.

GIANT YARD SALE!!

Three families.

Old books.

New toys.

Lots of things to collect.

Come early for the best deals!

Evidence	Text Structure

Overview Using Text Features to Locate Information I

Directions and Sample Answers for Activity Pages

Day 1	See "Provide a Real-World Example" below.
Day 2	Read and discuss the front cover and title page. Then ask students to complete the sentences. (**1:** Benjamin Franklin. **2:** Sera Y. Reycraft. **3:** both have the title, author, and a picture. **4:** They have different pictures. **5:** life and accomplishments. **6:** Responses will vary.)
Day 3	Read and discuss the table of contents. Then ask students to answer the questions. (**1:** page 2. **2:** page 12. **3:** Chapter 4. **4:** Chapter 1. **5:** Responses will vary. **6:** Introduction and/or Summary.)
Day 4	Discuss the pictures and captions. Ask students to answer the questions under each title. Then ask them to write a new caption for one of the pictures. (**Reduce, Reuse, and Recycle:** yes, no. **Cesar Chavez:** yes, no. **Probability:** yes, yes. **Student's Caption:** Responses will vary.)
Day 5	Provide each student with a nonfiction book that includes a front cover, title page, table of contents, chapter headings, and captions. Ask students to use the book to complete the chart. Afterward, meet individually with students to discuss their results. Use their responses to plan further instruction and review. (Responses will vary.)

Provide a Real-World Example

◆ Select a nonfiction book with a front cover, title page, table of contents, chapter headings, and captions. Provide each student with a nonfiction book.

◆ Hand out the Day 1 activity page.

◆ **Say:** *Nonfiction books have certain text features. We use these text features to locate, or find, information in the book.*

◆ Hold up your book. **Say:** *First, I will look at the front cover. The front cover shows the title and author of the book.* Point to the title and author's name as you read them aloud.

◆ **Say:** *Look at your book. Does your book have a front cover? Read the title and author's name to a partner. Then put a check mark in the front cover box on your chart. Then write on the chart what each feature tells you about your book.*

◆ Repeat the process for the remaining text features, first pointing one out in your book and then asking students to see if it is included in their books. Discuss their findings.

◆ **Say:** *This week we will learn more about these text features.* Write the following on chart paper:

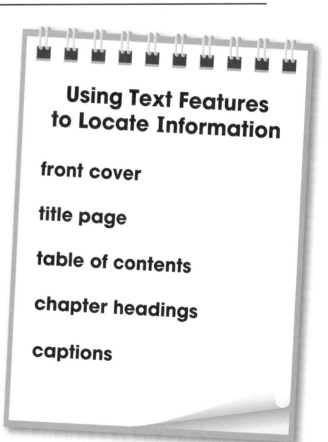

Using Text Features to Locate Information

front cover

title page

table of contents

chapter headings

captions

My Book

Choose a nonfiction book. Then write what each feature "tells" you about the book.

front cover	
title page	
table of contents	
chapter headings	
captions	

Front Cover and Title Page

**Look at the front cover and title page.
Then complete the sentences.**

Benjamin Franklin

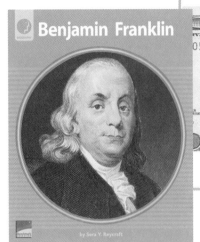

by Sera Y. Reycraft

Title Page

Front Cover

1. The title of the book is

   _____.

2. The author is

   _____.

3. The front cover and title page are alike because

   _____.

4. The front cover and title page are different because

   _____.

5. The book will probably be about Benjamin Franklin's

   _____.

6. Another good title for this book might be

   _____.

Table of Contents and Chapter Headings

**Look at the table of contents. Read the chapter headings.
Then answer the questions.**

A Whaling Community: Nantucket
by Vickey Herold

Table of Contents

1. On what page will you
   begin reading the book? _____

2. What page would you go to if you
   want to learn about whales? _____

3. Which chapter might tell places people
   like to visit in Nantucket? _____

4. Which chapter might have a map of Nantucket? _____

5. What is one thing you might read about in Chapter 2?

   _____

6. Where would you find information about the whole book?

   _____

Captions

A caption tells more information about a picture.
A caption can also ask a question.
Read each caption. Then mark **Yes** or **No**.

Many people recycle cans, glass, plastic, and paper.

Title of Book: *Reduce, Reuse, and Recycle*

Does this caption tell more about the picture?   **Yes No**

Does this caption ask a question?   **Yes No**

Title of Book: *Cesar Chavez*

Does this caption tell more about the picture?   **Yes No**

Does this caption ask a question?   **Yes No**

Cesar Chavez was awarded the Presidential Medal of Freedom.

Title of Book: *Probability*

Does this caption tell more about the picture?   **Yes No**

Does this caption ask a question?   **Yes No**

Choose one of the pictures. Write a new caption.

_____

_____ .

What is the probability that you will get "heads" if you flip this quarter?

Assessment

Use your book to complete the chart.

	Where did I find it in the book?	What is one thing I can learn from this text feature?
front cover		
title page		
table of contents		
chapter heading		
caption		

Overview Using Text Features to Locate Information II

Directions and Sample Answers for Activity Pages

Day 1	See "Provide a Real-World Example" below.
Day 2	Read the sidebars together. Then ask students to rate the sidebars and explain their ratings. (Responses will vary.)
Day 3	Read and discuss the passage and glossary. Then ask students to answer the questions. (**1:** glossary. **2:** swampy, marshy habitats. **3:** hot, dry habitats with tall grass and few trees. **4.** alphabetical. **5:** animal habitats around the world. **6:** Responses will vary.)
Day 4	Read and discuss the index. Then ask students to answer the questions. (**1:** page 7. **2:** pages 10–11 and 16. **3:** area, measuring, square feet. **4:** in alphabetical order. **5:** planting a garden. **6:** Responses will vary.)
Day 5	Provide each student with a nonfiction book that includes a sidebar, boldfaced words, a glossary, and an index. Ask students to use the book to complete the chart. Afterward, meet individually with students to discuss their results. Use their responses to plan further instruction and review. (Responses will vary.)

Provide a Real-World Example

◆ Select a nonfiction book with sidebars, boldfaced words, a glossary, and an index. Provide each student with a nonfiction book.

◆ Hand out the Day 1 activity page. Review the text features from the previous unit. Invite students to mark their charts to show which ones are included in their books.

◆ **Say:** *Nonfiction books have other text features, too. One text feature is a sidebar. A sidebar tells more about the information in a book.* Point out several sidebars in your book and read them aloud.

◆ **Say:** *Look at your book. Does your book have sidebars? Choose one to show your partner. Then put a check mark in the sidebar box on your chart.*

◆ Repeat the process for the remaining text features, first pointing one out in your book and then asking students to see if it is included in their books. Discuss their findings.

◆ **Say:** *Let's add these new text features to our chart.* Display the chart created in the previous unit and add the remaining text features to the list:

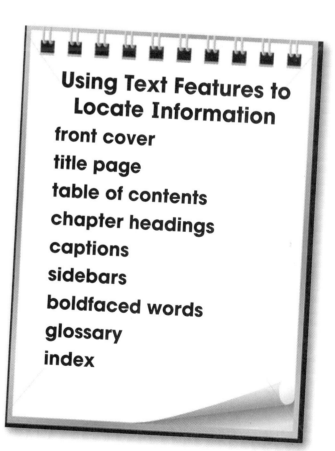

Using Text Features to Locate Information
front cover
title page
table of contents
chapter headings
captions
sidebars
boldfaced words
glossary
index

Front to Back

Choose a nonfiction book. Then write what each feature "tells" you about the book.

front cover	
title page	
table of contents	
chapter headings	
captions	
sidebars	
boldfaced words	
glossary	
index	

Sidebars

A sidebar tells more information about a person, animal, place, object, or event. These sidebars are from a book called *Human Emotions*. Rate each sidebar. Then explain your rating.

This sidebar is:

___good

___fair

___poor

I chose this rating because:

_____

_____.

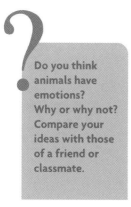

This sidebar is:

___good

___fair

___poor

I chose this rating because:

_____

_____.

Boldfaced Words and Glossary

Read the passage. Look at the boldfaced words. Find the words in the glossary. Then complete the sentences.

flamingo

Flamingos wade around in swampy **wetlands**. You would never see one in the **Arctic** or bounding across the African **savannas**. The special kind of place where an animal lives is called the animal's **habitat**.

3

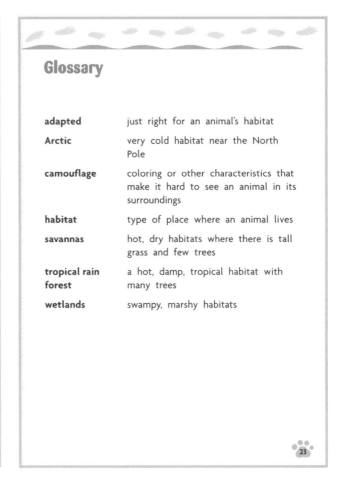

Glossary

adapted	just right for an animal's habitat
Arctic	very cold habitat near the North Pole
camouflage	coloring or other characteristics that make it hard to see an animal in its surroundings
habitat	type of place where an animal lives
savannas	hot, dry habitats where there is tall grass and few trees
tropical rain forest	a hot, damp, tropical habitat with many trees
wetlands	swampy, marshy habitats

23

1. The boldfaced words are also in the _____.

2. The first boldfaced word means _____.

3. The third boldfaced word means _____.

4. The words in the glossary are in _____ order.

5. This book is probably about _____.

6. A good title for this book might be _____.

Index

Look at the index. Then answer the questions.

1. On which page will you find information about marigolds? _____

2. What pages would you go to if you wanted to read about garden maps? _____

3. What is page 5 about?

   _____

4. How are the words in the index arranged? _____

5. What is this book probably about?

   _____

6. What might be a good title for this book?

   _____

Index

area, 5, 9, 13	perimeter, 17
budget, 3, 14–15	seedling, 3, 8–9, 11, 14–16, 20
cubic feet, 13	seeds, 3, 8–9, 11, 14–16, 20
fence, 17	soil, 12–13, 16
fertilizer, 3, 13	square feet, 5, 9–11, 13
garden store, 8–9, 14–15, 19	squash, 6, 9, 11, 15
insects, 7	stake, 19
lettuce, 6, 9, 11, 15, 20–21	thinning, 20
map, 10–11, 16	tomato, 6, 9, 11, 15, 19, 21
marigolds, 7	vegetable, 2–3, 6, 8, 14, 21
measuring, 3, 5, 13, 16	volume, 13
peat moss, 13	water, 16, 18
pepper, 6, 9, 11, 15	weeds, 12, 18

Assessment

Use your book to complete the chart.

	Where did I find it in the book?	What is one thing I can learn from this text feature?
sidebar		
boldfaced word		
glossary		
index		

Overview Using Graphic Features to Interpret Information I

Directions and Sample Answers for Activity Pages

Day 1	See "Provide a Real-World Example" below.
Day 2	Discuss each illustration and why the author might have used it instead of a photograph. Then ask students to color the circle in front of the best reason. (**Cell:** It shows parts we could not see in a photograph. **Sacajawea:** It is from long ago when people didn't have cameras. **Smokey Bear:** It shows something someone imagined.)
Day 3	Discuss each labeled diagram. Then ask students to circle the facts they learn. (**Insect:** An insect has six legs. The middle of an insect's body is the thorax. An insect has three main body parts. The end of an insect's body is the abdomen. **Water Cycle:** Rain runs off land into water. This is the water cycle. Rain falls from a cloud. Rain moves from the ocean back into the air.)
Day 4	Discuss the maps and their special features. Then ask students to complete the sentences. (**First Map:** Hawaii, California, Nevada, Utah, Wyoming, and Montana/Salt Lake City/Montana. **Second Map:** Europe/Africa/Atlantic/Indian.)
Day 5	Read the name of each graphic feature. Then ask students to use the graphic features to complete the chart. Afterward, meet individually with students to discuss their results. Use their responses to plan further instruction and review. (Responses will vary.)

Provide a Real-World Example

◆ Select a nonfiction book with photographs and inset photos. Provide each student with a nonfiction book.

◆ **Say:** *Nonfiction texts have graphic features. Readers must know how to interpret, or figure out, the information in a graphic feature. One important graphic feature is a photograph. We can learn a lot from a photograph!*

◆ Share some photographs from your book and what readers can learn from them. Point out any inset photos as well, noting how they provide additional details about the larger photograph. Then invite students to look through their own books and find a photograph to share with the group.

◆ Hand out the Day 1 activity page and discuss the photograph. Ask students to write words and phrases that tell what they learn from the photograph on the lines around it.

◆ **Say:** *This week we will learn about some other graphic features, too.* Write the following on chart paper:

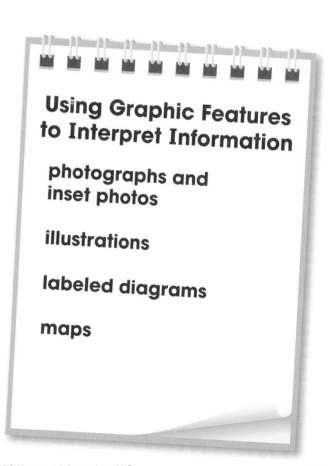

Using Graphic Features to Interpret Information

photographs and inset photos

illustrations

labeled diagrams

maps

Photo Search

Look at the picture. Then write about what the picture "tells" you.

_____   _____

_____   _____

Illustrations

Some nonfiction texts have illustrations. Look at each illustration. Think about why the author used an illustration instead of a photograph. Then color in the circle in front of the best reason.

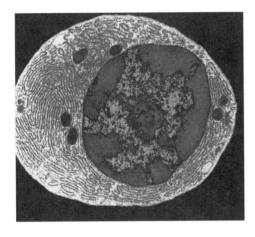

○ It is from long ago when people didn't have cameras.

○ It shows parts we could not see in a photograph.

○ It shows something someone imagined.

○ It is from long ago when people didn't have cameras.

○ It shows parts we could not see in a photograph.

○ It shows something someone imagined.

○ It is from long ago when people didn't have cameras.

○ It shows parts we could not see in a photograph.

○ It shows something someone imagined.

Labeled Diagrams

Look at each labeled diagram. Draw a circle around the facts you learn from the diagram.

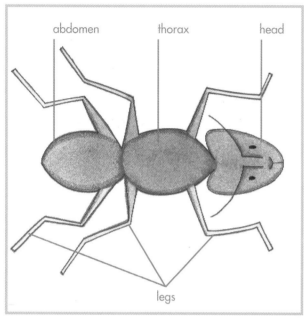

insect

An insect has six legs.

An insect has six main body parts.

The middle of an insect's body is the thorax.

An insect has three main body parts.

An insect has three legs.

The end of an insect's body is the abdomen.

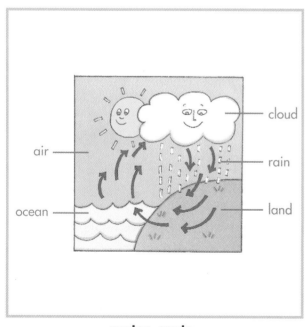

water cycle

Rain runs off land into water.

This is the water cycle.

The sun does not affect the water cycle.

Rain falls from a cloud.

Water moves through the water cycle quickly.

Rain moves from the ocean back into the air.

Maps

Look at each map. Then complete the sentences.

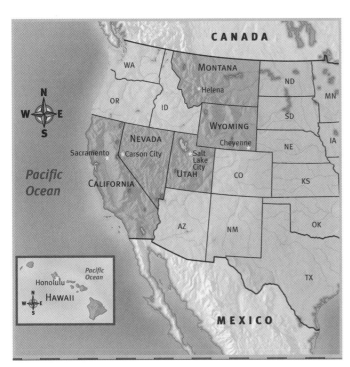

This is a map of the western states in the United States.

The western states are

_____.

The map names the capital of each western state.

The capital of Utah is

_____.

The compass rose shows the directions on the map.

The state that is farthest north is

_____.

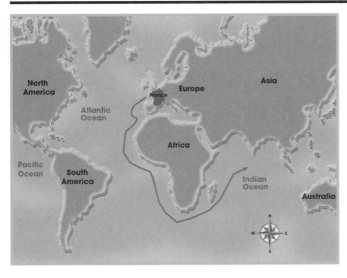

This map shows six of Earth's continents and the country of France.

France is in the continent of

_____.

Long ago, people from France wanted to sail to Asia.

The people sailed around

_____.

First, the people sailed through the

_____ Ocean.

Then the people sailed through the

_____ Ocean.

Assessment

Look at each graphic feature. Then complete the chart.

		What is one thing I can learn from this graphic feature?
photograph		
illustration		
labeled diagram		
map		

Overview Using Graphic Features to Interpret Information II

Directions and Sample Answers for Activity Pages

Day 1	See "Provide a Real-World Example" below.
Day 2	Read and discuss the table and its special features. Then ask students to answer the questions. (**1:** deciduous forest. **2:** at least 80 inches (200 cm). **3:** tropical rain forest. **4:** deciduous forest. **5:** between the North Pole and tropics and between the South Pole and tropics. **6:** birds, snakes, and insects. **7:** tropical rain forest. **8:** vines.)
Day 3	Read and discuss the weather station chart. Ask students to complete the sentences. Then discuss the hobby chart and allow time for students to complete it and share their results. (**1:** November 23. **2:** November 22. **3:** November 22 and 25. **4:** November 22 and 23. **5:** November 24.)
Day 4	Read and discuss the pie graph and bar graph. Then ask students to circle the facts they learn. (**Pie Graph:** Africa has over twice as many people as South America. Asia has more people than any other continent. The fewest number of people live in Antarctica. **Bar Graph:** Chocolate melts easier than plastic. The melting point of rock is over ten times higher than the melting point of chocolate. Ice melts at 33 degrees Fahrenheit.)
Day 5	Read the name of each graphic feature. Then ask students to use the graphic features to complete the chart. Afterward, meet individually with students to discuss their results. Use their responses to plan further instruction and review. (Responses will vary.)

Provide a Real-World Example

◆ Hand out the Day 1 activity page.

◆ **Say:** *We have learned that nonfiction texts have graphic features. Another graphic feature is a time line. A time line shows things that have happened and when they happened.*

◆ Ask students to look at the time line on the page. **Say:** *This time line shows different types of cars from long ago. The first period on the time line is the 1890s. Two brothers named Charles and Frank Duryea built the first American gas-powered car in the 1890s. Draw a line from the 1890s on the time line to the picture of the Duryea.*

◆ Repeat the process with the other dates and buildings (Early 1900s—Ford Model T; 1930s—Cadillac; 1950s—Ford Thunderbird; 1960s—Volkswagen "Beetle"). Then discuss how the time line helps show the history of cars.

◆ **Say:** *This week we will learn about some other graphic features, too. I will add the new graphic features to our chart.* Display the chart created in the previous unit and add the remaining graphic features to the list:

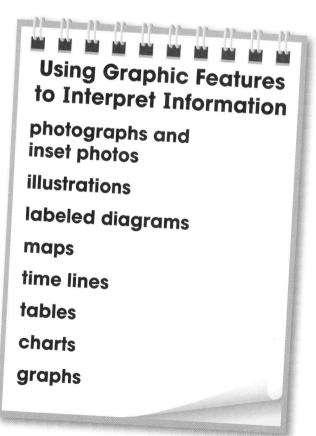

Using Graphic Features to Interpret Information

photographs and inset photos

illustrations

labeled diagrams

maps

time lines

tables

charts

graphs

Name _____

Cars

Look at the time line.

What does the time line "tell" you?

1890s

Early
1900s

1930s

1950s

1960s

Cadillac

Volkswagen "Beetle"

Duryea

Ford Thunderbird

Ford Model T

Forest Table

A table shows information that stays the same. Read the table. Then answer the questions.

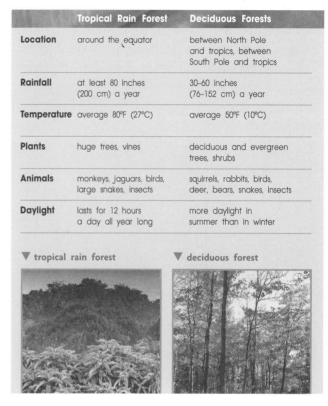

	Tropical Rain Forest	Deciduous Forests
Location	around the equator	between North Pole and tropics, between South Pole and tropics
Rainfall	at least 80 inches (200 cm) a year	30–60 inches (76–152 cm) a year
Temperature	average 80°F (27°C)	average 50°F (10°C)
Plants	huge trees, vines	deciduous and evergreen trees, shrubs
Animals	monkeys, jaguars, birds, large snakes, insects	squirrels, rabbits, birds, deer, bears, snakes, insects
Daylight	lasts for 12 hours a day all year long	more daylight in summer than in winter

▼ tropical rain forest   ▼ deciduous forest

1. Which type of forest has more daylight in summer than in winter?

   _____

2. How many inches of rain does a tropical rain forest get in a year?

   _____

3. Which type of forest is warmer?

   _____

4. Which type of forest has shrubs? _____

5. Where can you find deciduous forests? _____

6. What types of animals do tropical rain forests and deciduous forests have in common?

   _____

7. Which type of forest is located around the equator? _____

8. What type of plant does a tropical rain forest have that a deciduous forest doesn't have? _____

Charts

A chart shows information that can be different from day to day. Look at the weather station chart. Then complete the sentences.

Weather Chart					
Date	Time	Temperature in Sun	Temperature in Shade	Amount of Rainfall	Wind or No Wind?
November 22	1:00 P.M.	52°	42°	none	no wind
November 23	1:15 P.M.	48°	40°	none	wind
November 24	1:10 P.M.	no sun	47°	1/2 inch	wind
November 25	1:00 P.M.	no sun	51°	1/4 inch	no wind

1. The coldest day was _____.

2. The warmest day was _____.

3. _____ and _____ had no wind.

4. _____ and _____ were sunny.

5. _____ had the most rainfall.

Hobby Chart

A chart shows information that can be different from person to person. Fill in the hobby chart. Then share your chart with a classmate.

	Yes	No
read		
write stories		
cook or bake		
ride bikes		
skateboard		
play sports		
play video games		
make crafts		
do volunteer work		

Graphs

A graph is another way to show information. Look at the pie graph and bar graph. Draw a circle around the facts you learn from each graph.

Africa has over twice as many people as South America.

The combined population of Australia and Europe is more than the population of Africa.

Asia has more people than any other continent.

South America has more people than North America.

The fewest number of people live in Antarctica.

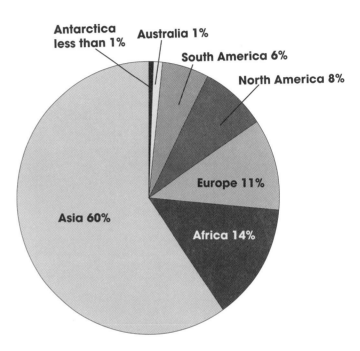

World Population by Continent

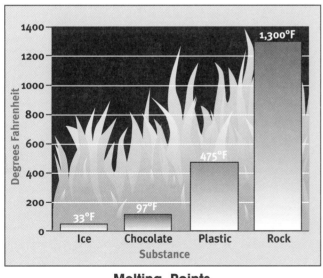

Melting Points

The chart only needs to go up to 1200 degrees.

Chocolate melts easier than plastic.

The melting point of rock is over ten times higher than the melting point of chocolate.

The greatest difference in melting points is between ice and plastic.

Ice melts at 33° Fahrenheit.

Assessment

Look at each graphic feature. Then complete the chart.

		What is one thing I can learn from this graphic feature?
time line	**From candles to compact disks** ▼ ▼ ▼ 1762 1886 1930 sandwich soda pop chocolate-chip cookie	
table	**New Zealand Bills** $5 orange $10 blue $20 green $50 purple $100 red	
chart	**Weekly Chores** Wash dishes Dad Weed garden Mom Feed Spot Manny Take out trash Tiana	
graph	Rainfall (in inches) in India during Monsoons Bombay Calcutta New Delhi August	

Notes

Notes